JESSE JAMES

Historical American Biographies

JESSE JAMES

Legendary Outlaw

Roger A. Bruns

Enslow Publishers, Inc.

40 Industrial Road
Box 398
Berkeley Heights, NJ 07922
USA

PO Box 38
Aldershot
Hants GU12 6BP
UK

http://www.enslow.com

Library of Congress Cataloging-in-Publication Data

Bruns, Roger.
    Jesse James : legendary outlaw / Roger A. Bruns.
       p. cm. — (Historical American biographies)
    Includes bibliographical references and index.
    Summary: Traces the life of the renowned bandit, from his childhood
in Missouri, through his years as guerrilla fighter and outlaw, exploring the
development of his legend and the romanticization of his illegal deeds.
    ISBN 0-7660-1055-4
    1. James, Jesse, 1847–1882—Juvenile literature. 2. Outlaws—West
(U.S.)—Biography—Juvenile literature. 3. Frontier and pioneer life—
West (U.S.)—Juvenile literature. 4. West (U.S.)—History—
1860–1890—Juvenile literature. [1. James, Jesse, 1847–1882.
2. Robbers and outlaws. 3. Frontier and pioneer life—West (U.S.)
4. West (U.S.)—History.] I. Title. II. Series.
F594.J27B78 1998
978'.02'092—dc21
[B]   97-24615
                                           CIP
                                           AC

Illustration Credits: Corel Corporation, p. 9; Enslow Publishers, Inc.,
pp. 15, 32, 80; Library of Congress, pp. 14, 31, 37, 47, 53, 55, 56, 76,
87, 90; Reproduced from the *Dictionary of American Portraits*,
Published by Dover Publications, Inc., in 1967, pp. 18, 58, 113; National
Archives, pp. 27, 73, 85, 91, 103, 107.

Cover Illustration: Corel Corporation (Background); National Archives
(Inset).

Contents

1

"HE STOPPED THE GLENDALE TRAIN"

At dusk on October 8, 1879, several people in the small farming town of Glendale, Missouri, were sitting around a store, swapping stories and talking about issues of the day. Suddenly, they found themselves in the middle of an event that would be talked about for years to come. Several men flashing pistols rode up to the store and ordered the people to march to the train depot. No one resisted. When the group reached the train station, one of the armed men began smashing the telegraph equipment.

The men asked the railroad agent in the depot to lower the signal to stop an incoming train. The train was not scheduled to make a stop at Glendale, so

Where Is Glendale?

In many histories of Jesse James and his gang, the town of Glendale is described as being just outside St. Louis. There is a Glendale in suburban St. Louis, but it is not where Jesse James robbed a train. That Glendale was located in Jackson County, southeast of Independence, Missouri, on the old Chicago and Alton Railroad in the western part of the state.

the agent at first refused. One of the thugs jammed the muzzle of his cocked revolver into the agent's mouth. The agent obeyed. The signal was dropped. The gang piled rocks on the track to wreck the train if it failed to heed the stop sign.

At exactly 8:00 P.M., a train approaching from the west sounded its whistles and rolled into the station. The outlaws, blasting shots into the air on both sides of the train, quickly rounded up the train crew. Passengers in the train cowered.

Inside the express car, an agent opened the safe and unloaded its contents into a bag, hoping that somehow he could escape. Before he could jump off the train, one of the outlaws beat him over the head with the butt of his revolver. With the contents of the safe in their possession, the bandits released the prisoners and escaped into the darkness.

Across the Midwest, newspapers blazed headlines about the robbery. Residents of Glendale, the men working on the train, and passengers who witnessed the robbery all began telling and retelling their stories. With each retelling, the stories changed slightly. The ferocity of the outlaws, the courage of the people involved, the intensity of the drama they had experienced in their own lives all

Jesse James and his gang became infamous as some of the first western outlaws to commit daring train robberies.

seemed slightly unreal now. It was excitement and terror and a day they would surely never forget.

Townspeople later talked about a note left by the gang. "We are the boys who are hard to handle," the note said, "and we will make it hot for the boys who try to take us." There was no question in the minds of the people in Glendale, Missouri. That night at the railroad depot, they had come face to face with the legendary Jesse James.[1]

2

GROWING UP IN THE STORM OF WAR

In 1842, a Baptist preacher and farmer named Robert James and his wife, Zerelda, left their native state, Kentucky. They settled in Clay County, Missouri, a farm area of fairly well-to-do families. The land settled by the James family was near the small town of Kearney, twenty-seven miles from Kansas City.[1]

There the couple built a log cabin and cleared some land for a farm. Robert became pastor of the New Hope Baptist Church. He later helped start the William Jewell College in nearby Liberty, Missouri. By 1850, Robert James held title to nearly three hundred acres of land and owned a small herd of sheep, several head of cattle, a few horses, and oxen. The family also owned seven slaves.[2]

In 1843, Robert and Zerelda celebrated the birth of a son. They named him Alexander Franklin James. As years went by, the first name did not seem quite right to family and friends; everyone began to call the boy Frank. In 1845, Zerelda gave birth to a second son, whom they named Robert. The boy died in infancy. Two years later, on September 5, 1847, another child arrived, also a boy. His name was Jesse Woodson James. In 1849, Zerelda gave birth to a girl, Susan Lavenia James.[3] The James family had grown quickly.

James McGuire was a friend who went to grammar school with Jesse and Frank James. Later, he reminisced about those early years:

> Yes, I know Frank and Jesse James. Now don't misunderstand me. I never was with them in their meanderings or maraudings, but we were raised in the same community and as young fellows, they were pretty good boys. . . . We had a favorite swimming hole in the Missouri River and it became a favorite spot for us on the hot summer days. It was a favorite trick of Frank's to throw mud on Jesse when he came out of the water.[4]

Although the James family was relatively well-off, Robert James had greater dreams for his family. He had read stories in local papers and heard from travelers passing through Missouri about gold strikes in

California and about sodbusters like himself suddenly becoming wealthy. California gold—perhaps this was the way to bring real riches to his family.

In 1850, Robert headed west with the same gold-fever dreams held by thousands who had gone before him. In April of that year, he closed a letter to Zerelda with these words: "Give my love to all inquiring friends and take a portion of it to yourself and kiss Jesse for me and tell Franklin to be a good boy and learn fast."[5]

Robert James never returned. He became ill and died of pneumonia in the California goldfields. Zerelda was left a widow. About five feet eight inches tall and weighing over two hundred pounds, she was strong, outspoken, and very protective of her children.[6] Zerelda married a second time, to a man named Benjamin Simms, but it was an unhappy union. The two separated, and he was killed in an accident shortly afterward.[7]

Her third marriage, in 1855, was to a doctor named Reuben Samuel. Four children were born to Reuben and Zerelda: Archie, John, Sallie, and Fannie.

Little is known about the boyhood lives of Jesse and Frank James. Nevertheless, their family, along with others in the Midwest, faced an uncertain future in a country racked by political division and

The James house in Kearney, Missouri, did not seem a likely place for one of the most notorious bandits in history to grow up.

hatred. It was those times, just before the Civil War, that helped shape character and change lives.[8]

On the Verge of War

During Jesse's childhood, the region was already torn by conflict over the question of extending slavery into new territories. For years, Northern and Southern politicians had fought over the issue.

In 1854 the delicate balance between the supporters and opponents of slavery had been violently shaken by the passage of the Kansas-Nebraska Act.

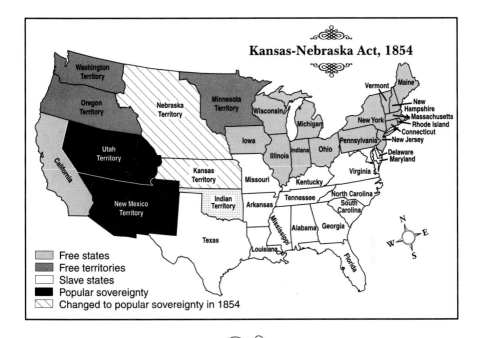

The Kansas-Nebraska Act of 1854 allowed the residents of new territories to decide for themselves whether to allow slavery within their borders. This map shows how the states and territories were affected by the Act.

Under the law, residents of new territories would decide for themselves whether to allow slavery—a system called popular sovereignty.

This idea seemed fair and democratic on the surface. However, the competition between the two sides over the future of the territory of Kansas and surrounding areas turned the region into a bloody combat zone. Antislavery leaders recruited new settlers to the region who did not want slavery. Southern proslavery leaders recruited proslavery settlers. *The Democratic Platform*, a proslavery newspaper published in Liberty, Missouri, called for slaveowners to move into Kansas with muskets in hand and prepare to die for the cause: "Shall we allow . . . cutthroats and murderers . . . to settle in the territory adjoining our own state? No!"[9]

The result was chaos—lynch mobs, random killings, and guerrilla violence. Many began to call the territory Bleeding Kansas. The dispute over slavery that flared there was only a preview of the bloodbath that was to erupt in the nation a few years later.

Antislavery and proslavery thugs and raiders clashed often and violently. Antislavery forces (called jayhawkers) raided towns in Kansas and in the neighboring slave state of Missouri, especially on border communities near Kansas City. They robbed and murdered and burned property.

Proslavery raiders pulled off equally violent attacks. They made daring raids into antislavery communities, suddenly appearing, striking, and then disappearing, taking to the woods or to the bush. People began to call them bushwhackers.[10]

Thus, a whole generation of children on the Kansas-Missouri border grew up seeing brutality and death. Some of them ended up carrying guns and knives and living for the next violent escapade. They were, in effect, undergoing training for the great war that followed.

The Outbreak of War

On December 20, 1860, a state convention in South Carolina declared that the union between that state and the rest of the states was dissolved. South Carolina had left the United States. Ten other states would soon follow South Carolina. The stage was now set for the great conflict between North and South, the Civil War.

In the Midwest, the hostilities between proslavery, pro-Confederate Missourians and antislavery, pro-Union Kansans had gotten worse. Gangs of Kansas antislavery thugs set fire to towns and farms in Missouri; bushwhacker guerrilla bands from Missouri retaliated.[11]

The state of Missouri would remain loyal to the Union. However, the James family owned slaves. Like many other families in Clay County, Missouri, the Jameses were decidedly pro-Southern. Jesse's mother was outspoken in her allegiance to Southern rights, especially on the matter of slavery.[12]

A group of Clay County residents seized rifles and small cannons from the federal arsenal at Liberty in early May 1861. Those arms made their way into the hands of people in the area. The communities began to form local militias to protect themselves against federal assault. Among the boys who joined one of those units was Private Frank James. He was eighteen years old.[13]

The Violent Career of William Quantrill

Frank and Jesse James would not make their mark in the Civil War by fighting with local militias in Missouri. They would have far greater roles to play. The man who would lead them was William Clarke Quantrill.

A native of Ohio, William Quantrill had been roaming around the Midwest working at various jobs in the summer of 1858, two years before South Carolina and the other states left the Union. For a time he drove horses and prospected for gold. Befriending an assortment of gamblers and gunslingers, Quantrill was soon stealing horses and rustling cattle.[14]

When Quantrill wandered farther southwest,

he was fascinated with the combat techniques used by the so-called guerrilla fighters of the Cherokee tribes. The guerrillas were small teams of warriors who

William Quantrill was the leader of a fierce band of guerrilla fighters who supported the Confederate armies during the Civil War. At a young age, Jesse James became one of Quantrill's raiders.

would make surprise attacks on the enemy and then disappear. It was these techniques that Quantrill would later use as his own. His gentle face and his soft blond hair disguised an ever-growing, intensely fierce obsession with military strategy and an attitude of nonchalance toward violence.[15]

On a cold December day in 1860, in Osawatomie, Kansas, four jayhawker abolitionists set off to Jackson County, Missouri. Their goal was to free the slaves of a well-to-do farmer named Morgan Walker. But one of the four men was an imposter. He was leading the others to their deaths. When the four reached the Walker home, an ambush awaited. On the front porch of the house, at the signal from the betrayer, a blast of gunfire swept through the bodies of the three unsuspecting victims. According to one account, one of the men survived the first blasts of the shotguns, but he did not survive a revolver blast through his mouth. The revolver was fired by the betrayer, William Quantrill.[16]

Quantrill was an eager participant when the Civil War broke out. He gathered around him men with fierce loyalty to the South, organizing a guerrilla band. Attack quickly and ferociously, he taught his men. Strike fear into the enemy and then vanish into the countryside. The guerrillas were not part of the Confederate Army, but on some occasions they worked with the Confederates. On August 11, 1861, Quantrill's men helped Confederate troops seize a federal garrison in Independence, Missouri. Quantrill's operations against Union forces later earned the guerrilla leader a captain's commission in the Confederate Army as head of Confederate Cavalry Scouts. He began to earn pay from the Confederate government.[17]

Even more bold because of his formal recognition by the Confederacy, Quantrill drove his fighters on to new conquests in Missouri and Kansas. Making bandit raids on small-town stores and banks, he slashed his way through Arkansas and Tennessee into Kentucky. The force never grew to more than fifty men, but it struck terror wherever it went.

At Olathe, Kansas, the raiders killed a dozen men. At Shawneetown, Kansas, another twenty, mostly civilians, were killed. An observer at Shawneetown talked of the horror of seeing men shot down "like so many dogs."[18]

Near Independence, Missouri, the raiders ambushed and killed Missouri militiamen. At Westport they killed nearly two dozen cavalrymen. Across the Midwest, Union and Confederate soldiers alike talked about Quantrill's campaign of violence and terror. Even soldiers on the Confederate side were shocked. One Confederate called Quantrill's tactics "savage and inhuman . . . in which men are to be shot down . . . after throwing down their arms and holding up their hands supplicating [begging] for mercy."[19]

The Youngers

Close to the James farm in Kearney, Missouri, lived four brothers who had left home and settled on their own. Their names were Coleman (Cole), James, John, and Robert Younger. The James boys and the Younger boys became close friends in their early teenage years. The violence in the region over the slavery issue touched their lives deeply. They listened to the stories of relatives and friends about the killings, burnings, and treachery of the enemy antislavery forces. They saw people close to them murdered and wounded.

Frank James and Cole Younger rode off with William Quantrill in 1862. Later, Jesse James rode off with one of Quantrill's lieutenants, a man whose nickname was Bloody Bill.

When Cole Younger joined Quantrill, he was eighteen years old. When Frank James joined, he was twenty. Sandy-haired, blue-eyed, with a square jaw and wide ears, Frank James was about five feet ten inches tall and slender.[20]

During their first few months with the guerrillas, Frank and Cole engaged in several encounters with Union troops. Several of the youngsters in

Quantrill's band were killed; nevertheless, they killed an even greater number of their enemies.[21]

Cole's father, Colonel Henry Younger of Harrisonville, Missouri, had been for several years a county magistrate and had served a few terms in the state legislature at Jefferson City. A man of extensive wealth, Colonel Younger owned thirty-five hundred acres of land in Jackson and Cass counties.[22]

Although Colonel Younger was proud of his Southern heritage, he had remained loyal to the Union. In late 1861, however, a group of antislavery men swaggered into Harrisonville and stole many of his possessions, including some forty horses. The prominent Missourian, insulted to the core, switched sides. He started supporting the Confederacy.[23]

The following summer, a few months after his son Cole had joined Quantrill's raiders, Henry Younger returned from a trip to Kansas City. On the road near his home, he was killed by a group of Union militiamen. Cole wanted revenge.[24]

Bloody Bill

"Bloody Bill" Anderson also rode with Quantrill's raiders. It was alongside Bloody Bill that Jesse James would get his baptism as a guerrilla fighter. Anderson's family had moved to Kansas from

Missouri in 1857. His father and mother had brought along their three sons and three daughters. The Council Grove area offered the family rolling prairies and relative quiet and serenity. But the war changed all that.

The Andersons refused to join the Union forces when the war began. In May 1862, Bill Anderson's father was killed in a bloody gunfight. Like Cole Younger, Bill Anderson seethed with a desire for revenge.[25]

Anderson soon formed a gang of several proslavery men to get that revenge. The area around Council Grove became a haven for Southern sympathizers and gained the reputation of being a rebel town. Bill Anderson helped make his father's town safe for bushwhackers. From this base of operations, he led groups of raiders through eastern Kansas. They burned houses and shot local Union sympathizers.

But once again, the Anderson family suffered. In early August 1863, a squad of Union soldiers captured Anderson's mother and sisters and escorted them to a prison in Kansas City. Within two weeks, the old, poorly constructed prison building collapsed, crushing one sister to death and permanently injuring another. Bill Anderson burned even more for revenge.[26]

He became known as Bloody Bill. There were stories of Bill's scalping Union soldiers and tying the scalps to his horse's bridle. Many enemies of the Union cheered him on. One Confederate woman from Missouri wrote to her brother on Christmas Day, 1863, "I thought for a while he acted brutal but now nothing he does can be too bad with me. I now laugh when I see the scalps of the Feds [Union soldiers] tied to the bridle bits."[27]

The Lawrence Massacre

From the early days of the war, the proslavery guerrillas had talked about a grand attack on the town of Lawrence, Kansas. Lawrence was the home of several antislavery leaders. To the raiders, burning the town would be a great conquest. They wanted the symbolic victory of burning down the center of abolitionism. The raiders knew the alarm that would fill eastern newspapers when Lawrence was in ashes. They thought of the joy in the slave states when word spread of this glorious victory.[28]

In early August 1863, Quantrill revealed his plan to hit Lawrence to his fellow guerrillas. Some of the men hesitated. But several days later, word arrived that the prison in Kansas City had collapsed, killing one of Bill Anderson's sisters. The bushwhackers agreed that it must have been a Union plot. All doubts about whether to attempt the dangerous attack on Lawrence were swept away in angry promises to punish and avenge.[29]

At dawn on August 21, 1863, William Quantrill, Bill Anderson, Frank James, and a huge force of approximately four hundred fifty guerrillas charged into Lawrence with their guns blazing. They killed men and boys, sparing only women and girls. For four hours the raiders wreaked havoc on the town. They burned and maimed in a wild frenzy of violence, screaming obscenities all the while.

Townspeople ran anywhere they could find safety, anywhere to escape the slaughter. They ran into cornfields, hid in chicken coops, ducked into outhouses, and crawled under wooden walkways. One man quickly put on a dress and bonnet and walked along with a group of women. There were scores of stories that hideous morning in Lawrence—of heroic attempts to save friends; of luck that led to life or death; of three thousand people trying to fend off the savage, long-haired riders invading their town.[30]

A Voice from Lawrence
A resident of Lawrence stated after the Quantrill massacre: "Lawrence is as much destroyed as though an earthquake had buried it in ruins."[31]

At least one hundred fifty men died that morning in the most devastating guerrilla raid of the Civil War. By the time the raiders left Lawrence, the town was a smoking inferno, with dead humans and horses smoldering along with crumbling wooden buildings.[32] A newspaper reporter estimated that one hundred twenty-five houses had been burned down.[33] Thomas Carney, governor of Kansas, wrote, "No fiends in human shape could have acted with more savage barbarity than did Quantrill and his band."[34]

An Order to Evacuate

Brigadier General Thomas Ewing, Jr., was commander of the Union forces in the area of Kansas and Missouri. Ewing responded to the Lawrence massacre with an extraordinary order. Residents of Jackson County and two adjoining counties were to be sent out of the area. Many of the guerrilla fighters lived there. The guerrillas' friends who had been sheltering and feeding them would be removed. This would cleanse the region so that the marauders would have less chance to survive.[35]

Thousands of men, women, and children left their homes under the guard of Union soldiers. The citizens included the mothers, wives, and sisters of several of Quantrill's raiders. In late August 1863, a Missouri newspaper described "refugees passing

Jesse James is shown here wearing his guerrilla uniform.

through our streets, ill clad, often times barefooted, leaving their only shelter, and their only means of substance during the approaching winter."[36]

With their relatives and neighbors being herded from their homes, Quantrill, Anderson, Frank James, and the other guerrillas decided on even greater violence.[37] Quantrill headed south toward Texas. In October 1863, near Baxter Springs in southeastern Kansas, the guerrilla fighters, dressed in blue Union Army uniforms, surprised federal cavalry units under the command of Major General James G. Blunt. In a fight that lasted from noon until almost dusk, Quantrill's force overran the Union troops, killing over eighty men. The cocky Quantrill was seen after the bloody battle drinking whiskey and toasting his success.[38]

He taught many things to his raiders: to strike suddenly and with force; to overwhelm their enemies not only physically but also psychologically; and to

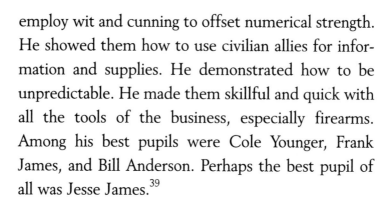

A Young Missouri Citizen

Following William Quantrill's raid on Lawrence, Kansas, Brigadier General Thomas Ewing, Jr., issued General Order No. 11. The order forced the residents of three Missouri counties to leave their homes. Among those forced to leave was an eleven-year-old girl named Martha Young. Years later Martha would give birth to future United States President Harry S Truman.

employ wit and cunning to offset numerical strength. He showed them how to use civilian allies for information and supplies. He demonstrated how to be unpredictable. He made them skillful and quick with all the tools of the business, especially firearms. Among his best pupils were Cole Younger, Frank James, and Bill Anderson. Perhaps the best pupil of all was Jesse James.[39]

3

THE BOY GUERRILLA FIGHTER

For many young rowdy boys, the Civil War was liberating. Armed with shotguns and Colt revolvers, dodging from one skirmish to another, the Quantrill and Anderson bushwhackers flourished. They found allies among the local people, who hid them in barns and fields and fed them food and information.

Frank James added a new recruit to Quantrill's raiders—his brother. Jesse James was a tough kid who had watched the Union militia beat his stepfather nearly to death. Jesse himself was once caught in a field by Union soldiers and flogged with a bullwhip. The violence in the nation was escalating. It profoundly shaped the lives of the James brothers.

Jesse James signed on as a guerrilla when he was seventeen. Blue-eyed and thin, he looked even younger than his age. He often batted his eyes, a condition brought on by a childhood eye affliction.[1] Through the summer of 1864, Jesse rode with Bloody Bill Anderson. An excellent horseman, Jesse was skillful with guns and seemed to be fearless. One of the guerrillas later said that Anderson was fascinated that a young kid like Jesse was perhaps the best fighter of the entire group.[2]

On September 26, 1864, the band terrorized the community of Centralia, Missouri, fifteen miles from Columbia. They set fires, robbed a stagecoach, and robbed and beat passengers from an incoming train.

The guerrillas then turned their attention to twenty-five unarmed Union soldiers who had been on the train. The raiders forced the soldiers to turn over their uniforms. They would use them later for disguises. Then they killed the soldiers one by one.[3]

A few days later, the raiders slaughtered nearly one hundred fifty Union militiamen in the same area and killed their commander, Major A.V.E. Johnson. Frank James credited his brother Jesse with the killing of Major Johnson.[4]

Guerrilla raiders caused panic and fear during the bloody years of the Civil War. This cartoon, "A Guerrilla Raid in the West," by the artist Thomas Nast, shows the widespread fear caused by the guerrillas.

For Jesse and the others, there were few restraints. For these Missouri Confederates, killing a Union militiaman was a patriotic duty. To Quantrill's raiders, butchery apparently was also. "The war has furnished no greater barbarism," said one stunned Union general.[5]

Crushing the Guerrillas

In October 1864, it all ended for Bloody Bill. He was killed outside Richmond, Missouri, in a gruesome cavalry battle. The dead guerrilla leader, still

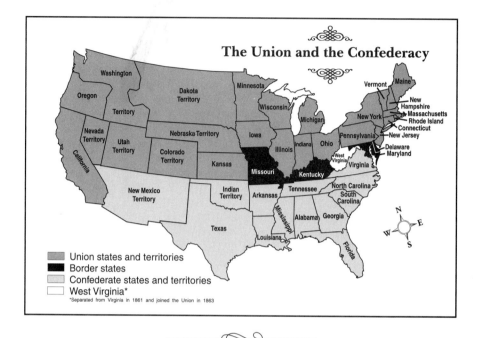

The Civil War split the nation. This map shows the states and territories, as they were divided in loyalty between the Union and the Confederacy.

clutching his Colt revolver, was beheaded. His head was mounted on a telegraph pole.[6]

A few days earlier, at a small battle near Independence, many of Quantrill's remaining fighters perished along with some regular Confederate troops. In Missouri, as in most parts of the United States, the grand cause of the Confederacy seemed to be lost.[7]

Headlines in Northern newspapers screamed for the blood of the butcher Quantrill. A newspaper reporter for the *Louisville Courier* called him a murderer who committed "acts of wantonness and wickedness."[8] The Union Army was determined to destroy him.

Captain Edwin Terrill, a former Confederate soldier, led a Union force into Kentucky to track down the infamous guerrilla leader and his men. Quantrill was now going by the name of Captain Clarke. He had always tried the unexpected. Never be predictable, he taught; always stay two or three moves ahead.

But in May 1865, near Bloomfield, Kentucky, Quantrill was brought down with a bullet in the back, which paralyzed his legs. He was found unconscious, his face in the mud.[9] He died in a military prison hospital in Louisville, Kentucky, several weeks later. He was twenty-seven years old.[10]

Frank James and the other survivors who had been with Quantrill in Kentucky surrendered to federal authorities. They were released after they took the oath of allegiance to the United States. Weary and humiliated, Frank James returned to Missouri.[11]

On April 9, 1865, Confederate General Robert E. Lee surrendered to Union General Ulysses S. Grant in a private residence in Appomattox Court House, Virginia. The Civil War was almost over.

Jesse James also made his way home. While on the road toward Kearney, he was shot in the chest by Union troops. The bullet punctured his right lung. For many months, he was quite weak. His survival seemed doubtful. But Jesse was soon attending Sunday services in church with his mother. During the week, he passed the time with other guerrilla veterans. They would tell stories of battles and keep their hatred of the Union hot. Jesse was restless. He craved more action.[12]

A Robin Hood

A song about William Quantrill described the murderous guerrilla as a hero. In the song, Quantrill was a "bold, gay, and daring" outlaw. He was called a Robin Hood from the mountains who descended with his band to the prairies to rob the rich and divide it "with widows in distress."[13]

Quantrill had done none of those things. But in the history of the West, this Robin Hood–hero myth emerged over and over again. Not only Quantrill would become a Robin Hood. Jesse James would become the greatest Robin Hood of them all.

4

THE RISE OF THE BANDIT KING

The story of Jesse James's outlaw career has been told and retold over generations. With each new telling, the stories of Jesse and Frank James and their bandit gang have become more exaggerated. Their deeds have become more noble.

The career of Jesse James has been set to music. It has been written about in novels and short stories and presented on television and radio. It has been the subject of paintings. His life has been turned almost completely into myth and legend. Jesse James has become as much a part of American culture as other folk heroes, from Daniel Boone to Paul Bunyan.

During the Civil War, thousands of men and boys like Jesse James became accustomed to lives of fighting and surviving on the run. Their best friends were the war buddies with whom they banded together. They liked the freedom; they liked the wildness and the adventure. They craved the violence and the near escapes. Even though they had seen death, many of them still felt invincible.

In the relatively unsettled and raw towns of the frontier, the population was scattered. There was little law enforcement. Here, Jesse James and others tried to keep living as if the war had never ended.

Many Confederate bushwhackers believed they were still not whipped by the Union. They continued to fight for what they saw as the grand cause. Ex-guerrilla fighters rode into old abolitionist towns like Abilene and Dodge City, Kansas, and raised all kinds of trouble. When the citizens brought in professional gunfighters to wipe out the rowdies, they usually called for ex-Union soldiers, men like Wild Bill Hickok, Wyatt Earp, and Bat Masterson.

In Missouri especially, the ex-Confederate boys held forth after the war. Jesse and Frank James, like many other former Confederate soldiers and guerrilla fighters, had no desire to settle down on their farms to a tedious life and meager existence under the control of the Union government. For them, the war had meant power and the excitement of uncertainty and chance.

Although Quantrill was dead, Jesse and Frank James, and others, would continue their own personal wars. The ex-Confederates would begin to rob banks and then trains, which were mostly owned by Northerners. Many Southern sympathizers would cheer them on and protect them from local sheriffs, many of whom were ex-Union soldiers.[1]

Jesse James and others would still be guerrillas. They would still use the small-gang, hit-and-run

The western frontier after the Civil War was an unpredictable and often dangerous place, where former guerrillas could easily continue their violent deeds. This is how the West was depicted in Harper's Weekly *magazine in 1865.*

attacks they had learned from their Civil War leaders. James would always scout the countryside for hidden valleys where they could hide and pasture their horses. He would keep an eye open for caves in which bands of men could hide for days and even weeks. He and the former guerrillas would continue their own war and make the raider life a profession. They would make names for themselves, make money, and never surrender.[2]

Target: The Banks

Jesse and Frank James continued to live in Kearney with their family after the war. The quiet family farm did not seem to be a likely birthplace for the nation's most notorious bandit.[3]

On Tuesday afternoon, February 13, 1866, the Clay County Savings Bank in the small college town of Liberty, Missouri, was robbed. Historians consider this robbery, by a gang of about a dozen ex-Confederate raiders, the first successful daylight bank robbery during peacetime in the United States.[4]

The outlaws rode into Liberty from different directions and gathered in front of the bank. Two of the men got off their horses and entered the bank. The others stayed on their horses outside and, according to reports of witnesses, seemed to be nervous as they waited for the robbery, which took ten to fifteen minutes, to be finished. Two men were working inside the bank: head cashier Greenup Bird and his son and assistant, William. One of the outlaws asked to have a bill changed. As William approached the counter, the robbers drew their guns and demanded all the money. The first man handed William an empty feed sack from under his coat. Once the money, bonds, and tax stamps were placed in the feed sack, the outlaws forced both Greenup and William Bird into the vault.[5]

The outlaws were dressed in military blue coats and wore other Union Army items. However, the disguises did not fool several of the local townspeople, who knew some of the robbers. As the men left the bank and began to mount their horses, a commotion took place. One man seemed to be having some problems with his horse. Amid confusion and panic, wild shooting erupted in the streets. A young college student was killed in the middle of the

The Cashier Remembers

According to the account of Greenup Bird, cashier of the Clay County Savings Bank, Liberty, Missouri, on the bank robbery of February 13, 1866, "On his arrival at the counter, the man on the opposite side drew a revolver and presented it at Wm. Bird and demanded the money of the Bank."[6]

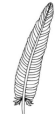

chaos. The boy had been attending William Jewell College, the institution that Jesse and Frank James's father had helped establish.

Yelling curses and firing their guns wildly, the gang charged out of Liberty. At a safe place, they counted their day's "earnings," which totaled about $100,000.[7] An article in a Liberty newspaper declared, "The murderers and robbers are believed . . . to be . . . old bushwhacker desperadoes" who should be "swung up [hanged] in the most summary manner."[8]

The robbery at Liberty occurred when Jesse James was still recovering from the chest wound he had suffered at the end of the war. It is likely that Frank James participated in the robbery and that Jesse had some role in planning it. The exact role of the James brothers will never be known, as no one was ever convicted of committing the robbery.[9]

In the following months, bandit gangs struck other banks in the Missouri towns of Lexington, Savannah, and Richmond.

His chest still not completely healed, Jesse and Frank James, and the Younger brothers decided to hide out at the home of the Jameses' aunt, Nancy Hite, near Adairsville, Kentucky. While in hiding, Jesse James was treated by a doctor specializing in chest wounds. Over the next several months, he slowly regained his strength.[10]

Jesse and Frank James, Cole Younger, Jim White, John Jarrett, and George Shepherd, all of whom had been members of Quantrill's guerrilla raiders during the Civil War, decided to rob the Southern Deposit Bank of Russellville, Kentucky, on March 20, 1868. The outlaws entered the bank and asked the cashier, a man named Nimrod Long, to cash a bond. The men then drew their guns and leaped over the bank counter. Long ran out of the room. The outlaws shot at him, but he escaped, only being grazed by a bullet. One of the bank assistants loaded a sack. Estimates of the gang's take range from $9,000 to $14,000. After the robbery, they again fled to the Hite home near Adairsville to hide from authorities.[11]

Law enforcement officials in the area formed posses. They interviewed victims and followed trails, but they were unsuccessful in tracking down the violent thieves.[12]

Although Jesse and Frank James had ridden with some of the men accused in the robberies, law authorities had no evidence at the time that either of the James brothers was involved. Nevertheless, lawmen were on the trail of some of the Jameses' former guerrilla friends. The lawmen were ready to catch the fugitives and find a nearby tree on which to hang them.[13]

On some occasions, the residents of towns hit by the bandits did not wait for the lawmen to act. Two nights after the Richmond, Missouri, robbery, in an especially vicious encounter in which the mayor of the town was gunned down, a mob broke into the town jail. The mob dragged out a man named Felix Bradley, and hanged him from the limb of a tree at the edge of town. Bradley, who was in jail for another crime, probably had nothing to do with the robbery. He had mentioned to his fellow prisoners that the bank would be robbed before the day was over on the same day that the robbery occurred. For this, he probably became a target for the mob.[14]

Other executions in the region followed. A former Quantrill raider named Thomas Little was also suspected of involvement in the Richmond robbery. Little was dragged from his cell in the Jackson County jail by residents of Warrensburg, Missouri, and hanged. Soon, two other ex-Quantrill guerrillas were hunted down by mobs and murdered.[15] In March 1868, two more ex-raiders held as robbery suspects in Richmond, Missouri, were hauled out of their cells and hanged from nearby trees. The Richmond jail was rapidly becoming one of the least safe spots in America.[16]

On December 7, 1868, two men robbed the Daviess County Savings Bank in Gallatin, Missouri. One of the men calmly shot a bank official through the head and heart. He then wounded another bank employee.

During the bandits' escape, townspeople opened fire. The bandit who murdered the cashier was unable to mount his excited horse. Tangled in the stirrup, he was dragged a short distance. After he freed himself, he crawled on the back of another horse and managed to leave town, relatively unhurt, with his two fellow gunmen. A short distance out of town, the outlaws stole another horse and headed south toward Clay County.

The abandoned horse was eventually traced to the James home in Clay County. As a posse approached the farm, two men on horseback charged out of the stable and escaped after a brief gun battle. The posse was convinced that the two men were Jesse and Frank James.[17]

Although the James brothers denied responsibility for the crime, they refused to turn themselves in to the authorities for trial. Few people believed their claims of innocence. They were now directly linked to robbery and murder. They were now fugitives.[18]

Early in their bank robbing careers, it became clear that the leader of the bandits was Jesse James—not Frank or any of the Younger brothers. Jesse James was skillful at plotting strategy, picking out the most likely targets, and organizing the gang. He also was the most energetic. He went at the outlaw business with remarkable flair and imagination. He even sent letters to local newspapers denying that he was responsible for various bank robberies. "I have lived as a peaceable citizen, and obeyed the laws of the United States to the best of my knowledge," he wrote to a Kansas City newspaper after the Gallatin affair.[19]

Making the Outlaw Business Look Easy

In June 1871, the James gang hit a bank in the small Iowa town of Corydon. They picked a time when many of the townspeople would be gathered on the courthouse grounds to hear a famous speaker named Henry Clay Dean. Dean was talking about the possibility of building a railroad through the town. After gathering up about $10,000 in cash and tying up the bank cashier, the gang rode onto the courthouse grounds. In front of Henry Dean and his audience, Jesse James asked to speak. Dean replied, "I yield to the man on horseback."[20] James told the crowd that the bank had been hit and that the cashier was tied up. He suggested that someone in the crowd might want to set him free. The gang then rode out of town.

In September 1872, the James gang struck the Kansas City Fair in Missouri at midday. They pulled off the brash robbery in the midst of several thousand fairgoers. The cocky guerrilla veterans rode their horses up to the ticket office, demanded the day's receipts—about $10,000—and left the fair firing shots into the air while they cleared a path through the excited and frightened crowd of people.[21]

Stories abounded about Jesse James's miraculous escapes. "One of the most daring escapes made by Jesse and Frank James was . . . in the early '70s," one Missouri man remembered:

> Officers giving pursuit shot the horse from under him [Jesse James]. He met his brother Frank on the other side of the river. Part of the way to the meeting place, Jesse walked a picket fence in order to keep bloodhounds from trailing him. When he joined Frank, the two journeyed on, Frank riding behind with the money. Soon they met a doctor driving a horse and buggy. They took his horse. A little farther on they met a Negro on horseback. They took his saddle and bridle. Jesse now had a horse and saddle, so they made their get-a-way.[22]

Jesse James's Devoted Promoter

To a journalist named John Newman Edwards, this kind of banditry was not terrible crime but the stuff of courage, bravery, and noble deed. Edwards was a former Confederate soldier. In the *Kansas City Times*, he compared the perpetrators of the Kansas City attack with ancient legendary figures like King Arthur and his Knights of the Round Table.

Through the years, Edwards would become the James gang's most enthusiastic defender and promoter. He claimed that the James gang would ride into western outlaw history. Edwards himself did what he could to see that prediction come true.

The robbery at Kansas City, Edwards said, was a crime; but it was a crime of such daring and fearlessness that it must be admired. The newspaperman wrote of the gang: "With them booty is but the second thought; the wild drama of the adventure first. These men never go upon the highway in lonesome places to plunder the pilgrim. That they leave to the ignobler [more vulgar] pack of jackals."[23] No, the James brothers, he said, rode in daylight, in the open, witnessed by the admiring public.

In the Kansas City robbery, a member of the James gang accidentally shot a small girl in the leg. Edwards, in his glowing tribute to James and his gang, chose to ignore this fact. His article on the gang was entitled "The Chivalry of Crime."[24]

Edwards always managed to convince himself and many of his readers that the James brothers were acting to defend their fellow citizens and their families against outrages committed against them. The bandits were, he claimed, strong men taking on the lawmen who were against the general population. The James gang, he said, still stood for a grand cause. They fought against those Northerners who had treated the people of the Confederacy so viciously.[25]

Edwards never changed his mind about Jesse James. He wrote frequent articles about the bandit,

LOG CABIN LIBRARY   (Pocket Edition)   10 CENTS

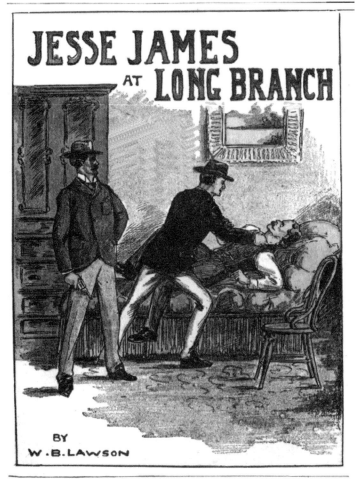

JESSE JAMES AT LONG BRANCH

BY
W.B.LAWSON

No. 14 { STREET & SMITH, Publishers,   29 Rose Street,
Mar. 16, '98 }   NEW YORK.

John Newman Edwards became a devoted supporter of the James gang. Through his books and other forms of popular entertainment, like this dime novel, the James brothers and their fellow bandits became an important part of American culture.

justifying James's outlawry in the name of Southerners. He also justified the outlaw's deeds in the name of manly valor. Jesse James's acts, said Edwards, were on behalf of those less fortunate than himself. Never, said Edwards, did James act for personal profit or glory.[26]

Edwards almost singlehandedly turned James into a glamorous figure. He made even his personal features admirable. James's face, said Edwards, was as "smooth and innocent as the face of a school girl. The blue eyes, very clear and penetrating, are never at rest. His form is tall, graceful and capable of great endurance and great effort."[27] At times, Edwards said, James "mingled the purr of the tiger with the silkiness of the kitten."[28]

Local Heroes

Across the Midwest, many citizens agreed with Edwards about the James boys. They were not feared criminals but heroes. They were not only carrying on the Confederate cause, but also attacking banks that were owned by wealthy Northerners.

The boys consistently drew attention to themselves. L. A. Sherman, a young butcher in Quincy, Illinois, remembered seeing the James brothers in a restaurant in his hometown:

> I was eating at an eatin' house in Quincy, Ill. [W]hen I had stuffed my fill and lit my pipe, I found out that one of the men eatin' there was Jesse James. Was I

scart [scared]. I wouldn't be eatin' a bite had I known Jesse was there. He carried two big revolvers on his hips. His brother Frank was there too. They often came to Quincy. . . . Strong. Frank had black hair. Black beard, that is a goatee. Jess had full beard, five inches long . . .[29]

Many midwestern ex-Confederates looked at James and his gang as local boys who had stood up against the rich businessmen of the North and won. Some of the community around Kearney considered Jesse and Frank James to be like family. Indeed, some locals actually were James family members. Jesse James recruited two of them—his cousins Wood and Clarence Hite—into the gang.

The local citizens hid the gang in barns and fed gang members in their kitchens. They helped Jesse James and his boys get away with murder and robbery for the better part of two decades. Most people in the region believed that no local jury would ever convict members of the James gang.[30]

The young butcher, L. A. Sherman, said,

By God, these times were hard. When these guys wanted money, they went in daylight to [take] their money. No one would dare shoot when they robbed a bank. . . . The James boys were liked by the poor and God knows there was plenty of us and the law made no serious effort to get them.[31]

5

TRAIN ROBBING

The railroads were moving west. Into Missouri and the surrounding states, the big, belching locomotives rolled across the prairies, moving people and goods at speeds many had never dreamed possible. On many of those trains were shipments of money. To Jesse James and his fellow gang members, the railroad presented new opportunities. The boys decided to add a new element to their robbing careers: they decided to hold up trains.

Train robbing was not an invention of the James brothers. A gang led by the four Reno brothers had robbed a train in Indiana in September 1866. But the James boys added their own twist to the art.

The Iron Horse Arrives
On May 10, 1869, the Central Pacific Railroad and the Union Pacific Railroad connected their rails at Promontory Point, Utah, just north of the Great Salt Lake. The United States now had a railroad line across the continent, from the Atlantic Ocean to the Pacific. For homesteaders, farmers, and ranchers—for all Americans—the giant, soot-belching trains brought new opportunity. For Jesse James, they brought new targets.

East of Council Bluffs and west of Des Moines, Iowa, the Chicago, Rock Island, and Pacific Railroad reaches Adair, Iowa. At this spot, on July 21, 1873, the James gang executed their first train robbery. The gang loosened a rail just before a locomotive approached the station. They attached a heavy cord to the rail and waited. When the train reached the spot, the boys pulled the rail. The giant engine rolled crazily into the cinders and spun awkwardly onto its side. The wreck crushed much of the train's engine and killed the engineer, John Rafferty. The passengers and other crew members were frightened and bruised but survived. The gang collected money from the train's safe and valuables from the passengers.[1]

The wreckage of the train was never removed. It still lies "buried" near the town of Adair today.[2]

Six months after the gang hit their first train, they decided on yet another type of target: stagecoaches. Hot Springs, Arkansas, was a favorite vacation resort that lured tourists with the reputed healing waters of the many thermal springs that flowed from the hills around the city. Wealthy resort visitors often arrived in the area on trains, and special coaches picked them up to carry them through the mountains to Hot Springs.

On January 15, 1874, a coach approached Sulphur Creek from the direction of Malvern. On board were fourteen passengers. Five men in long blue overcoats with handkerchiefs over their faces came out from behind the rocks and ordered the stage driver to stop at gunpoint. The gang forced the passengers out of the coach and lined them up. All of them were frisked for weapons and then told to kneel with their hands in the air. When one male passenger refused to keep his arms up, the bandits informed him that if he continued to disobey, he would be shot through the head. The passengers' money, watches, and jewelry were collected and placed in a grain sack. One of the passengers, an old man, told the robbers that he had been a Confederate cavalryman during the Civil War. Before leaving the scene, one of the outlaws, whom

Stagecoaches and trains were popular targets for bandits like the James gang. This is a Wells Fargo Express "treasure wagon," the type often hit by bandit gangs in the years after the Civil War.

many historians believe was probably Cole Younger, returned the man's money bag to him—a gesture, everyone assumed, that was intended to show solidarity with ex-Confederates. After unhitching and scaring away the team of horses from the coach, the robbers rode quietly away.[3]

In late January 1874, a little over two weeks after the gang's first stagecoach robbery, the boys hit another train. The scene of the action was at Gads Hill, Missouri, a small village on the Iron Mountain Railroad about a hundred miles south of St. Louis.

In the Gads Hill robbery, the outlaws, according to newspaper stories, asked to see the hands of the male passengers to see if they were "working men." If so, the outlaws did not rob them. They also, of course, did not rob the ladies.[4]

When the outlaws at Gads Hill were preparing to leave the scene, one of them handed the railroad engineer a written account of the story. All the newspapers had to do, he said, was fill in the blank space in the story with the correct amount of money. The story was titled, "The Most Daring Robbery on Record."[5] Jesse James had written, in advance of the robbery, his own press release of the event.[6]

When the James boys began their train-robbing adventures, the national press began to pick up the stories of the gang with even greater enthusiasm. The names of Jesse and Frank James and Cole, James, John, and Bob Younger were becoming familiar to readers in New York City, Boston, and Charleston, South Carolina. Some reporters, taking their lead from John Newman Edwards, portrayed these men as criminals driven to their deeds by wartime hatreds, and as men standing up for their own people against outside forces. They wrote of the gang members as heroes acting on principle and following a code of honor.[7]

LOG CABIN LIBRARY (Pocket Edition) 10 CENTS

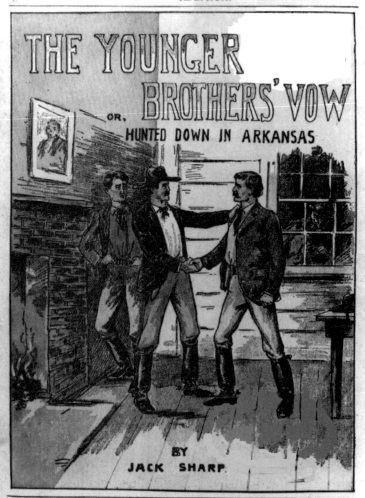

THE YOUNGER BROTHERS' VOW

OR, HUNTED DOWN IN ARKANSAS

BY
JACK SHARP

No. 15 }
Mar. 23, '98 } **STREET & SMITH, Publishers,** 29 Rose Street, NEW YORK.

Like the James brothers, the Younger brothers were frequently depicted in dime novels like this one.

Some of the news stories were exaggerations of actual incidents; others were totally made up. It was said, for example, that Jesse James once declared, "We never rob Southerners," and that he lived up to that promise. In fact, many of the individuals robbed by the James gang were Southerners.[8]

Jesse James's exploits were reported in *The Police Gazette*, a magazine read in barbershops, billiard rooms, and bars across the United States. His bank and train robberies became the stuff of

Bandits shoot it out with lawmen in Nebraska in an issue of The Police Gazette. *The* Gazette *often published news of incidents involving criminals like Jesse James and his gang.*

thrilling legends in cheap dime novels sold in drugstores and train stations.

The tall tales snowballed with each retelling. So many stories circulated about the gang that in several instances they were reported to have robbed banks, trains, and stagecoaches in different locations on the same day.[9]

The James and Younger brothers and their fellow gang members carried their work into Kansas, Kentucky, Iowa, and Texas. Sheriffs and marshals across the West had no luck trapping or even tracking the gang.[10]

For bank and train company officials, embarrassment piled on embarrassment. Their companies were losing money, and the body count of Jesse James's victims was rising. The company executives decided to put an end to James and his men. They called for hired guns. They called in the Pinkertons.

Bring On the Pinkertons!

The motto of Pinkerton's National Detective Agency was "We never sleep." Its symbol was an open eye. The agency was founded by Allan Pinkerton, an immigrant from Scotland who had started out in the United States as a barrel maker. Pinkerton later joined the Chicago police force and then started his own private detective agency in 1850.[11]

Allan Pinkerton was a Scottish immigrant who founded the first private detective agency in the United States. He was given the task of taking down the James gang.

From its earliest days, before the Civil War, Allan Pinkerton's agency brought in a multitude of criminals: forgers, pickpockets, safecrackers, diamond thieves, embezzlers, and wrongdoers of all kinds. Railroads and banks across the country gladly paid high prices to protect their interests.

The Pinkertons were smart and relentless. During the war, Allan Pinkerton, along with his two sons, Robert and William, and their other agents, did intelligence and protection work for the Union forces and for President Abraham Lincoln.[12]

By the 1870s, the agency's crime-solving precision had gained international fame. When Pinkerton agents took up the hunt for the James gang, they confronted even more difficulties than local law enforcement officials had faced. They were seen by much of the population as opportunistic thugs hired by the hated railroads, banks, and other corporations to put down the local gangs. They were outsiders in Missouri, venturing into unfamiliar territory. They had little personal knowledge of the habits, appearance, and tactics of the gang. Although they were trained professionals with a good reputation, the Pinkertons had not yet handled a task like bringing down the James gang.

The efforts of the Pinkertons to corral the James gang were not only unsuccessful but also tragic. In March 1874, one agent, attempting to get close to the gang to learn of their movements, tried to get hired to work at the James farm. Before he approached the farm, one local resident told him, "The old woman will kill you if the boys don't."[13] He was later found alongside a road near Independence, Missouri, with bullets through his heart and head.[14]

Shortly after the Pinkertons lost this agent, two other agents confronted several of the Younger brothers near Osceola, Missouri. The ensuing gun battle left both Pinkerton men dead. But the Youngers also suffered a loss. John Younger, shot through the neck with a pistol by one of the agents, fell from his horse, dead.[15]

The reputation of the Pinkertons was suffering at the hands of the James gang. The boys eluded the detectives and even found time for family life.

Jesse and Zee

Zerelda (Zee) Mimms of Kansas City, Missouri, was a first cousin to Jesse James. Born in July 1845, she was one of the twelve children of John W. Mimms and James's father's sister Mary James. On April 23, 1874, at her sister's home in Kearney, Zee was married to Jesse James by a Methodist minister in the presence of about fifty friends and relatives. James later wrote, "Her devotion to me has never wavered for a moment. You can say that both of us married for love, and that there cannot be any sort of doubt about our marriage being a happy one."[16]

A friend of the two described Zee as a beautiful young lady with a "face that would be attractive in any assembly."[17] The two headed south to Texas for their honeymoon.

An Assassination Attempt

With newspapers across the country questioning whether Pinkerton's National Detective Agency or any other organization could wipe out the legendary bandit king, the Pinkertons decided on a bold strike. On a frigid night in late January 1875, the Pinkertons attempted to assassinate the James brothers at their Clay County farm, or Castle James, as some of the local residents and Pinkerton agents called it. A posse of Pinkerton agents and county lawmen surrounded the darkened house, where they assumed the boys were spending the night. Posse members shouted for Jesse and Frank to surrender. They received no response.

In an effort to set fire to the house and force the occupants outside, the men lobbed a black-powder bomb through the window. It was made of a brass shell stuffed inside a kerosene-soaked gunnysack.[18] The James boys' mother and stepfather, Dr. Samuel, were inside with their nine-year-old son, Archie. When the flaming ball crashed through the window, Dr. Samuel shoved it into the fireplace. It exploded. The log cabin was engulfed in smoke. When the posse rushed in, they found Archie fatally wounded and Mrs. Samuel bleeding from a serious wound to one arm. Blood had spattered the walls. Mrs. Samuel lost much of her arm; young Archie lost his life.[19]

The events of those few minutes of botched law enforcement ensured that the Jesse James legend would grow to even greater proportions.

A newspaper declared, "There is no crime, however dastardly, which merits a retribution as savage and fiendish as the one which these men acting under the semblance of law have perpetrated."[20] John Newman Edwards, to no one's surprise, thundered his own outrage at the attempt to murder James and called for ex-Confederates to fight back at the Pinkertons: "Men of Missouri, you who fought under Anderson, Quantrill . . . and the balance of the borderers and guerrillas . . . give up these scoundrels to the Henry Rifle and Colt's revolver."[21]

Although other reporters across the country did not care to revive the Civil War over the incident, they did write many sympathetic columns to James and his family. A *New York Times* editorial declared, "Everyone condemns the barbarous method used by the detectives."[22] The *St. Louis Dispatch* said that all former guerrilla fighters who had turned to crime in desperation after the war must be pardoned for the crimes they committed during the war.[23]

Press indignation was mirrored early on by some members of the Missouri state legislature who, following the lead of the *St. Louis Dispatch*, introduced a bill providing for the pardoning of all ex-bushwhackers for their wartime deeds. But before the legislature acted on the measure, the James gang was apparently involved in the murder of a neighbor who was suspected of helping the Pinkertons. With public opinion about the gang divided, legislators rejected the bill.[24]

In their attitudes about the James gang, the public, the press, and the politicians all shared confusion and mixed sympathies. Jesse James and his friends sparked feelings of local pride, wartime bitterness, and fascination. At the same time, their wild deeds of violence also brought fear and disgust.

The Pinkertons, proud masters of detective craft, seemed to lose heart in the hunt for the James gang after the farmhouse episode. The agency quietly faded from the scene. When told that local residents in Clay County, Missouri, intended to arrest the Pinkertons for the killing of the boy and the maiming of the Jameses' mother, Allan Pinkerton reacted only with anger. He wrote that Jesse James's mother had "met with a merited and fearful punishment."[25] The Pinkertons expressed no remorse for any injury inflicted upon either the outlaw James brothers or their family, because of all the terrible deeds the James gang had done to others. Robert Pinkerton, one of Allan's sons, said later, "I consider Jesse James the worst man, without exception, in America."[26]

6

THE NORTHFIELD DISASTER

By late summer 1876, the James gang was at the height of its power. Seemingly invincible, the boys decided to take their robbing and murdering north. One of the gang members, Bill Chadwell (alias William Stiles), persuaded Jesse James and the others that his home state of Minnesota would be a rich hunting ground of easy banks.

On the morning of September 7, 1876, decked out in long linen coats, eight men approached Northfield, Minnesota, a prosperous community that had been settled mostly by pioneers from Norway and Sweden. The gang of eight included Jesse and Frank James; Cole, James, and Robert

Younger; Clell Miller; Charlie Pitts (alias George Wells); and Bill Chadwell.[1] It was a ride the James gang never should have taken.

Ten days before the planned bank robbery, two of the outlaws visited Northfield to get acquainted with its layout, especially the position of the bank. On the morning of September 7, the gang met in the woods five miles west of town and began to ride slowly into town. Their long linen coats concealed their guns and cartridge belts.

Around two o'clock in the afternoon, Jesse James, Charlie Pitts, and Bob Younger rode over the bridge and down the main street, dismounting in the front of the bank. After throwing their reins over some hitching posts, they walked down the street and sat on some boxes in front of a store. Shortly after, Cole Younger and Clell Miller rode onto the main street from the opposite direction.[2] As Younger and Miller rode slowly toward the bank, they noticed that a great number of people were milling around in the streets. Cole Younger later remembered "a crowd of citizens about the corners, also our boys sitting there on some boxes. I remarked to Miller about the crowd and said, 'Surely the boys will not go into the bank with so many people about.'" After Miller had confidently lit up a pipe, Cole Younger told him to put it out. Younger sensed that things were about to explode.[3]

When the three men sitting on the boxes saw the other two men approach the bank, they got up, leisurely strolled to the door of the bank, and walked in. After dismounting, Miller also walked to the bank while Cole Younger stayed in the middle of the street and pretended to tighten his saddle girth. As he had feared, all this movement around the bank seemed to attract the attention of several more citizens.

At the bank, the situation deteriorated quickly. J. S. Allen, the owner of a nearby hardware store, attempted to enter the bank but was grabbed by Miller, who told Allen to get back. Allen was able to pull away from Miller. He then ran back into the street, shouting, "Get your guns, boys. They are robbing the bank!"[4]

About the same time, a young medical student was sitting in front of his father's drugstore close to the scene. He saw Allen's encounter with Miller. He began to shout, "Robbery! Robbery!"[5]

With citizens yelling and screaming, Miller and Younger leaped onto their saddles. They began riding up and down the street. They were quickly joined by the other three gang members, who had been waiting at the edge of town. Citizens of Northfield hastily passed around guns and ammunition, deserted the streets, and closed the doors of stores and offices.

The outlaws and some of the townspeople began shooting. A Swedish man named Nicholas Gustavson, who did not understand English, remained on the streets after the bank robbers had told the townspeople to get away. Gustavson became the battle's first casualty. He died four days after he was shot.

One of the citizens, peering from around a corner of a building, took aim at Bill Chadwell on his horse, some seventy or eighty yards away. His shot ripped through the outlaw's heart. Chadwell slumped dead in his saddle. Another bullet blasted through Clell Miller, also killing him instantly.

Fleeing down the street on their horses, the rest of the outlaws faced a horrifying storm of shotgun, rifle, and pistol fire. From the windows of stores, from around corners of buildings, and from rooftops, bullets flew into Northfield's main street. A hailstorm of lead ripped into the ground, buildings, horses, and men. The scene of a robbery had turned into a war zone.

Inside the bank, the bandits encountered resistance from the bank employees, who refused to open the safe. One of the outlaws pushed a revolver in the face of the cashier, Joseph Heywood, and demanded that he open the safe. He refused and was slugged to the floor. Another bank employee then dashed toward the door and was shot in the right shoulder by Pitts, but he made it outside. In the street, one of the outlaws yelled to his comrades in the bank, "This game is up! Better get out boys, they are killing all our men." The gang members in the bank began to rush out. The last one that left shot Heywood through the head.[6]

Outside, Bob Younger's elbow had been shredded by a rifle blast. His horse was shot down. Cole Younger had been ripped apart, although none of the wounds proved fatal. One of Cole's friends later wrote about those few minutes on the street: "Cole felt a sting in his side, another high on his shoulder; his hat was shot away, the horn of his saddle was ripped loose and hung there—swaying in the wind."[7]

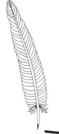

Citizen Hero

Joseph Lee Heywood became a local hero in Northfield. The thirty-nine-year-old bank officer was killed when he resisted the James gang's efforts to rob the First National Bank. Several banks from the United States and Canada contributed to a fund of over $12,000 for the benefit of the family and as a tribute to Heywood. Carleton College, of which he was also an officer, established a Heywood Library Fund in his honor, and there is a memorial plaque at Carleton. A memorial window in the United Church of Christ of Northfield also bears his name.

Six bandits—the three Younger brothers, Frank and Jesse James, and Charlie Pitts—managed to escape from the streets of Northfield into the countryside. But every one of the Youngers was seriously wounded.

The battle of Northfield had lasted about seven minutes. The bank's money was safe. In front of the bank lay a dead horse. Nearby were the bodies of Nicholas Gustavson and Clell Miller. Half a block away, on the other side of the street, was the body of Bill Chadwell. In the bank lay the body of Joseph Heywood.

The telegraph carried word through Minnesota that the Northfield desperadoes were on the run and wounded. Almost immediately after the robbers' escape, farmers, townspeople, and lawmen

Trying to Form a Posse

Law enforcement officials and private detective agencies hired to bring down the James gang had difficulty forming posses in Missouri. William Pinkerton talked of trying to get a deputy to help him: "He said he would . . . aid me secretly, but owing to the relatives and sympathizers of these men residing in the county he dared not lend me a hand openly."[8]

from around the state turned out by the hundreds to organize a manhunt to bring them down.

Drenched by hard rains, unfamiliar with the countryside, and suffering from terrible wounds, the gang wandered in circles in the western Minnesota wilderness. Three times that afternoon, small groups of the Northfield manhunt force nearly reached the fugitives. By that night, there were at least two hundred citizens involved in the search. The number of people looking for the robbers would eventually reach at least a thousand.[9]

The fugitives found a place to hide out on a small island in a swamp. They set up a camp there. They then traveled to an area about two miles from Mankato, Minnesota, where they found an abandoned farmhouse. They stayed there for two days and nights. After five days of wandering through the woods, the fugitives had traveled fewer than fifty miles from Northfield. Patrols and search parties closed in, guarding every possible avenue of escape night and day. Police officers came down from Minneapolis and St. Paul, Minnesota, to take part in the manhunt.

Jesse and Frank James separated from the others. The brothers stole a pair of gray horses and mounted them bareback. They traveled both day and night, riding west, and were able to cover eighty miles in two days.

The Younger brothers and Pitts, meanwhile, crossed the railroad bridge over the Blue Earth River near Mankato, where they were at last cornered by their pursuers. They were trapped in an area covered with a thicket of trees and brush. The two forces were only about ten yards apart. The fight was over quickly. In a weak exchange of gunfire, Pitts fell dead and the exhausted Youngers, ripped with bullet holes, their clothes bloodied and shredded, surrendered to the posse. Bob Younger weakly called out, "I surrender; they are all down but me."[10]

On September 17, the James brothers crossed the Minnesota border into the Dakota Territory. There they took Dr. Sidney Moshier, Sr., a Sioux City, Iowa, physician, prisoner. They made him treat Frank James's wounds. His left leg had been badly shot up at Northfield.

Miraculously, the Youngers managed to survive their massive injuries. On September 23, the prisoners were treated for their wounds and brought to the county jail in Faribault, Minnesota, to await trial. Newspaper reporters, photographers, detectives, and others hovered around the jail to get the latest words from the prisoners and to take pictures. As rumors circulated that citizens nearby were plotting to snatch the prisoners from the jail and hang them, law enforcement officers tightened security.

Interviewed by reporters, Cole Younger expressed regret for his crimes. He talked of his boyhood joy in attending Sunday school, quoted from the Scriptures, and wiped tears from his eyes. Some of his listeners were impressed.[11] At Northfield and at the skirmish in the swamp, the man had suffered a total of eleven bullet wounds and had survived. He would carry those bullets in his body for the rest of his life.

On November 9, the Youngers were arraigned in the Rice County district court. The grand jury charged them with the murders of Heywood and Gustavson, attacking other townspeople with deadly weapons, and attempting to rob the First National Bank. The Youngers pleaded guilty. The state laws provided that if a murderer pleaded guilty, capital punishment could not be inflicted upon him. The Youngers were sentenced to life in prison.

The Youngers served their sentences in the Minnesota State Penitentiary in Stillwater. Bob Younger told a reporter, "We tried a desperate game and lost. But we are rough men used to rough ways and we will abide by the consequences."[12]

After Northfield, the James brothers disappeared. They made it to the Dakotas, but their trail vanished near Sioux Falls. There is a story that the brothers stole two horses from a farmer's yard during the escape. One of the horses was blind in

This photograph of Jim Younger was taken while he was recovering from a gunshot wound to his face suffered at the Northfield, Minnesota, disaster.

one eye and the other was blind in both eyes. Despite their horses' limitations, the James brothers managed to ride many miles.[13]

Enemies and admirers alike tried to shed light on their movements and intentions. Some said they went to Mexico; others insisted they had headed west. Police and private detective agencies still had only vague descriptions of the outlaws—tall, bearded, lean—descriptions that, in the West of the 1870s, fit more than a few men. If Northfield, Minnesota, had been a disaster for the James gang, the James brothers had at least survived.

TAKING JESSE JAMES DOWN

For a couple of years after the disaster at Northfield, Jesse and Frank James merged into society, putting their outlaw careers on hold. The Youngers were gone. Other gang members had also been killed or jailed. Jesse James, the nation's most celebrated bandit, was lying low.

He and his brother avoided capture by living under assumed names in Nashville, Tennessee; St. Louis, Missouri; and other cities in the Midwest.[1]

A Growing Family

Jesse and Zee James had moved to the Nashville area in early 1875. Using the name John Howard,

Cole
Younger

Jesse
James

Frank
James

Bob
Younger
(rear)

The James Boys and the Younger Brothers

The Pinkertons and other law enforcement officials did not have photographs of the James gang. Over the years, many fake photographs circulated. This one has appeared in books and magazines for over seventy-five years.

Jesse James posed as a businessman. The house was situated on a knoll where James and Zee believed they could see the approach of posses on their trail. James slept near a window, from which he could leap if the house were invaded.

In December 1875, Zee had given birth to a son, whom they named Jesse Edwards. The name Edwards came from John Newman Edwards, the newspaperman whose stories had spread James's fame throughout the United States. Little Jesse's alias was Tim Howard.[2]

In 1879, Zee gave birth to a daughter, whom she and James named Mary. Years later, Mary told a newspaper reporter that as children she and her brother never knew that James was their real last name.[3]

Outlaws Again

While the James brothers took a rather lengthy rest from the outlaw business, they lived on what money remained from the bank and railroad robberies. They began to accumulate substantial debts—especially Jesse James, who lost money on racehorses. In the fall of 1879, James and his family moved back to Missouri. Word began to circulate that the famed outlaw was ready to form another gang.

Law enforcement officials heard the rumors. But even with Jesse James's nationwide fame, the outlaw remained a slippery fugitive. Sheriffs and Pinkerton men still did not have photographs of the brothers. The descriptions given by many of the gang's victims had been varied, not a surprising fact given the stress that the eyewitnesses had been under when they had gotten glimpses of the bandits.

On October 8, 1879, the gang struck. With the Youngers now in prison, the James brothers had taken on a few small-time robbers and horse thieves as partners. At dusk, several armed men wrecked the telegraph equipment at the Glendale, Missouri, railroad station, ordered the agent to signal the train to stop, and piled rocks on the tracks just in case the engineer ignored the signal. The train did stop. Firing shots wildly in the air to frighten the passengers, the outlaws broke into the express car and stole over six thousand dollars.[4]

Jesse James returned to settle down in Tennessee. But apparently the outlaw blood was still raging in his veins. The excitement, the danger, the fame, and rewards—it all must have been beckoning him once again. Although Frank James was less inclined to resume the life, he went along with his brother. The gang was, indeed, back in business.

On July 15, 1881, the boys robbed a Chicago, Rock Island, and Pacific train at Winston, Missouri. They killed the conductor with two bullets in the back, killed one of the passengers, and viciously beat several other individuals with their revolvers.[5]

It was now clear to almost everyone except the most enthusiastic Jesse James supporters that the bandit was no longer in the outlaw business to avenge the South—if he ever had been. The latest raids had nothing to do with the old bushwhacking days of the Civil War. They had nothing to do with punishing ex-Yankees or embarrassing bank and railroad interests because they were owned by Northerners. They had nothing to do with robbing the rich to somehow benefit the poor. They had to do with making money and keeping Jesse James's name in the papers.

In 1881, James moved his wife and children back to Missouri. They lived in St. Joseph in a rented house high on a hill.[6] From the beginning of his outlaw career, James had always enjoyed support from friends and neighbors. Many had cheered on the ex-Confederate guerrilla out of a sense of loyalty and friendship. Others had kept their silence about his outlaw activities out of fear. But at a trial of a James gang member in Jackson County, Missouri, an old Confederate stronghold, several witnesses revealed Jesse James's involvement in robberies. The prosecutor later said that the trial convinced many people in Missouri, who had been afraid to talk about the

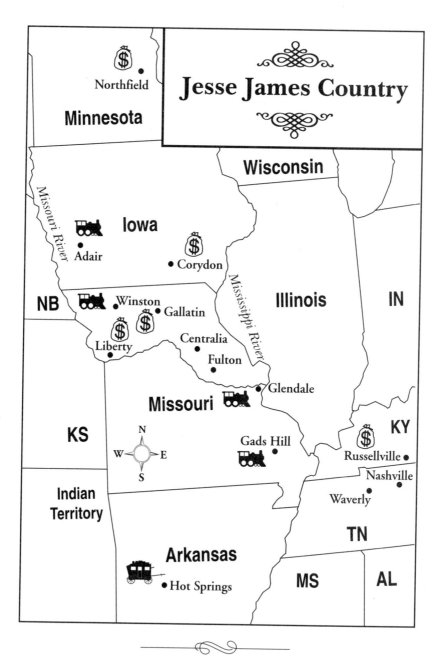

This map shows the areas in which the James gang committed its notorious robberies of banks, trains, and stagecoaches.

gang, that it was now possible to offer valuable information and still live.

The James boys had become, through the years, a major annoyance to railroad companies and an embarrassment to the state of Missouri. Indeed, many newspaper writers and politicians around the country were calling Missouri a home for outlaws. The James boys were again bad for business.[7]

Reward Money

In 1881, Governor Thomas Crittenden of Missouri decided to take vigorous action against the brothers. Meeting with railroad company officials in St. Louis, the governor attempted to raise a large amount of money for rewards to be paid for the capture of the James gang. Although state funds were limited, he thought railroad companies might donate some money.

The railroad executives had paid the Pinkertons and other hired guns to wipe out the James gang. All their efforts had failed. The executives enthusiastically agreed to Crittenden's requests. These were their terms: bring in the brothers and receive $5,000 a head, another $5,000 each for their conviction, and $5,000 more for the arrest and conviction of other participants in crimes of the James gang.[8]

Crittenden himself called upon citizens to bring down the James gang with all force necessary. He wanted them to chase the bandits "by day or by night, until the entire band is either captured or exterminated."[9]

In the fall of 1881, on the line of the Chicago and Alton Railroad at Blue Cut, east of Independence, Missouri, the bandits struck again. It was almost the same place they had hit another train two years earlier. They laid a pile of rocks and logs on the track to stop the train. Once aboard, they beat the express car messenger with pistol butts. The train's engineer later testified that the tall, bearded bandit leader, who wore no mask, shook his hand and gave him two silver dollars "for you to drink to the health of Jesse James . . ."[10] This added a little more spice to the legend. It had been nearly five years to the day that the gang had been shot up in Northfield, Minnesota.

But Governor Crittenden's reward offers had tempted two members of the James gang—Bob and Charlie Ford. Charlie had been along on the hit of the Chicago and Alton Railroad, and Bob was supposed to see his first gang action in a robbery scheduled for a bank in Platte City. The Fords, indeed, lusted for money, but not in the way Jesse James had in mind. Bob and Charlie Ford decided to turn James in for the reward.

Assassination as Planned

On April 3, 1882, at the house in St. Joseph, Missouri, where Jesse James lived with Zee and their two children, Bob and Charlie shared a meal with the outlaw. They talked about the next day's plans. James apparently remarked that the Platte City robbery would be his last and that he planned to take the family to Nebraska and retire on a farm.

When James took off his guns, laid them down, and turned his back to the brothers, apparently intending to dust off and straighten a picture, Bob Ford drew his Smith & Wesson .45 and shot the infamous outlaw through the back of the head.[11]

In the law of the Old West, few things were considered more cowardly than shooting an unarmed man in the back. As a folk song later told it:

> O *the people in the West, when they heard of*
> *Jesse's death,*
> *They wondered how he came to die.*
> *It was Ford's pistol ball brought him tumbling*
> *from the wall,*
> *And it laid poor Jesse down to die.*
>
> O *Jesse leaves a wife, she's a mourner*
> *all her life,*
> *And the children, they were brave,*
> *But the dirty little coward, he shot*
> *Mister Howard,*
> *And he laid poor Jesse in his grave.*[12]

The Bandit Hideout

In the 1880s, St. Joseph, Missouri, bustled with immigrants heading west and with commercial activity. It was an ideal hideout town for outlaws, and it was in a quiet St. Joseph neighborhood that Jesse James spent his last days. He had successfully hidden from the law; it was a fellow outlaw who brought him down.

Jesse James's body was soon seized by law enforcement officials, autopsied, and propped up on a board, as was the custom of sheriffs showing off their kill to the locals. The practice was to discourage others from engaging in a life of crime.

Immediate family members accompanied the body by train to nearby Kearney for burial. It was viewed by the entire James family and hundreds of onlookers who had known Jesse James as a boy. No one doubted that the body was actually that of Jesse James.[13]

A local grand jury at St. Joseph, Missouri, indicted the Ford brothers for James's murder, even though the governor of the state had offered a reward. On April 17, 1881, the brothers pleaded guilty and were sentenced to hang. That afternoon,

Bob Ford, the assassin of Jesse James, posed for this photograph with the weapon he used to kill the infamous outlaw.

Governor Crittenden received the news of the sentence by telegraph and immediately granted Bob and Charlie Ford full pardons.[14]

To newspaperman John Newman Edwards, the legend-builder and glorifier of the myth, James's death provided further material. Assassination by traitors, by plotters! What better way for an historical folk hero to perish? Edwards unleashed his untamed prose to do its work once again. "There was never a more cowardly and unnecessary murder committed in all America than this murder of Jesse James," Edwards wrote.[15] Jesse James, said Edwards, was like Julius Caesar, or even like Jesus, who was also betrayed by someone he trusted: "indignation . . . is . . . thundering over the land that if a single one of the miserable assassins had either manhood, conscience or courage, he would go, as another Judas, and hang himself."[16]

Editorialists railed against the blood bargain struck up between the governor of the state and cold-blooded killers. The unseemly plot darkened the history of Missouri, many said, even more than the black outlaw deeds of Jesse James.

Some refused to believe that James had died. Rumors and wild tales of devious plots and escape and a new life for the bandit would continue to color the Jesse James legend.

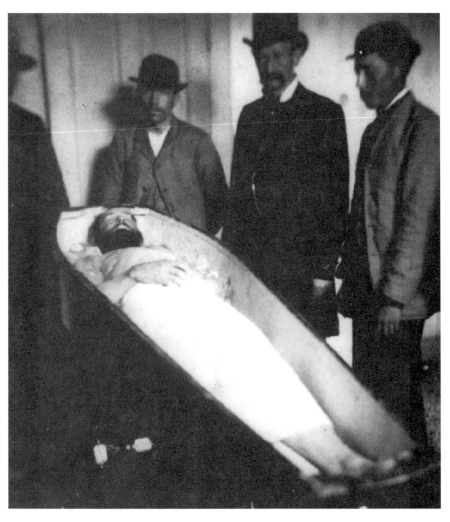

Mourners surround Jesse James's casket in this 1881 photograph. Many people refused to believe the outlaw had actually died, which added to the legend of Jesse James.

The Legend of Jesse James Grows

Soon after James's death, it was clear that the life of Jesse James had become a national legend. In late April 1882, *The Judge*, a satirical magazine in its first year of publication, proposed that a monument be built in James's honor. While depicting train and stagecoach robberies, the monument would also feature a model of James's home. Inside the house, amid guns, daggers, and revolvers, would be three plaques bearing the following messages: Bless Our Home, What Is a Home Without a Revolver, and What a Friend I Have in Jesus and my Revolver.[17]

In late summer 1882, in Springfield, Missouri, a blind woman stood in front of the courthouse singing an ode to Jesse James. It was a song composed by a man named Billy Gashade shortly after James's death. Passersby dropped coins in the blind woman's tin can. The woman was later slapped in the face and knocked down in the street by Bob Ford's sister, who did not like the lyrics, which treated Ford's act as a murder.[18]

A year later, Tootle's Opera House in St. Joseph, Missouri, opened a drama about Jesse James. The company featured a special onstage attraction—two horses that supposedly had belonged to the infamous outlaw. One horse, Roan Charger, had been identified by a local man as having been in James's stable, only yards from the room where the outlaw was gunned down by Bob Ford. The other horse, Bay Raider, had been one of James's racehorses, according to stage company spokesmen, though this later turned out to be a fraudulent claim.[19]

In February 1884, Bob Ford gave his side of the story about the assassination of Jesse James. In a letter to the editor of the *Missouri Republican*, Ford said that he had not made a deal with Governor Crittenden. He said: "I only did what thousands of others were trying to do but failed. . . . The man that calls me an assassin is a CONTEMPTABLE [*sic*] SNEAK . . ."[20]

Bob Ford later suffered the same fate as Jesse James. In a saloon he operated in Creede, Colorado, Ford was shotgunned to death by a man named Ed Kelly. The motive was unclear.[21] Ford's brother Charlie committed suicide a few years later.

Frank James, tired of the outlaw game, surrendered to Governor Crittenden at Jefferson City on October 5, 1882. Frank had decided to let the citizens of Missouri decide his fate. On two separate occasions, once at Gallatin, Missouri, and later at Muscle Shoals, Alabama, he stood trial. Each time, sympathetic juries, lacking hard, eyewitness evidence, voted for his acquittal. William Pinkerton, an old foe of the James brothers who had chased the gang unsuccessfully for years, wrote, "There is too much sympathy . . . for those cold-blooded killers."[22]

William Pinkerton, who had unsuccessfully chased Jesse James for many years, sits at his desk in Chicago at the turn of the century.

The James brothers had robbed banks, stagecoaches, and trains for many years. They had killed and maimed and created chaos in several states. They had drawn sheriffs and posses and professional detectives to their trail. Despite all this, the James brothers were never convicted of a single crime.[23]

In October 1892, in Coffeyville, Kansas, another gang of outlaw brothers—the Daltons—was brought down. During a crazy attempt to rob two banks at the same time, most of the Dalton gang

This photograph of Frank James was taken in 1898, sixteen years after the death of his brother, Jesse.

members were killed in the streets by townspeople. In an interview with the one surviving Dalton, Emmett, a reporter learned that the reason the boys had tried to rob two banks at the same time was that Jesse James had never done it. Emmett told the reporter that his brother Bob had "wanted to lower Jesse James' record."[24]

Frank James, old and weary of the whole crime business, turned to other pursuits. He sold shoes, got a job as a theater guard in St. Louis, and then worked as a horse race starter at county fairs. For a time, he accepted speaking engagements to lecture on the theme "Crime doesn't pay," all the while, of course, still trying to make it pay.

At the turn of the century in Kearney, Missouri, Jesse James's mother continued to decorate her son's grave at the homestead with flowers. People who supported Jesse James sent her flower seeds to help keep the gravesite well decorated. She entertained visitors (for a tourist fee) with tales of her outlaw sons. She perfected the performance, crying for her lost son and swearing revenge against the Pinkertons and others who had worked to stop the James gang. An extra twenty-five cents would get the visitor a few stones from Jesse James's grave to keep as a souvenir.[25]

In July 1901, Cole and James Younger received paroles and left the Minnesota state prison. Bob

Younger had died in prison of tuberculosis in 1889. James and Cole soon found jobs selling monuments for the Peterson Granite Company. James Younger, who had lost most of his jaw from wounds suffered at Northfield, fell in love with a writer named Alice Miller. Under the terms of his parole, the ex-outlaw was not allowed to marry. Despondent and ill, he ended his life in October 1902, with a shot through the head in a shabby hotel room in St. Paul.[26]

The James gang now had only two survivors. Cole Younger and Frank James, boyhood allies, reunited for a time in old age. In 1903, they formed the Cole Younger and Frank James Historical Wild West Show. The extravaganza featured, along with fake gunfights and horse stunts, a fake stagecoach robbery. It also included "Russian Cassocks, Bedouin Arabs, American Cowboys, Roosevelt Rough Riders, Indians, Cubans, Western Girls, Mexicans, Broncos, Overland Stage Coach, Emigrant Train, The Siege of Deadwood and the World's Mounted Warriors." The advertisement emphasized that Cole Younger and Frank James would appear personally at every performance.[27]

As the Wild West show toured the Midwest, it became an increasing embarrassment. The actors hired by Younger and Frank James constantly got into trouble with local sheriffs, often shooting guns at inappropriate places and getting into fistfights.

One newspaper added, "Such shows should, in our opinion, be suppressed. The younger generation sees men of world wide notoriety as criminals exhibited and hailed as heroes. The influence upon children is undoubtedly bad."[28]

Law enforcement authorities did not have to close down the show. Younger and James closed it down because it was not making money.

Frank James later moved back to the James farm, where he charged visitors fifty cents for a tour. He died in 1915 at the age of seventy-two. Cole Younger died a year later.

Neither Frank James nor Cole Younger was immortalized as a hero. Nor were any of the men who served time or grew old or took undignified jobs. The hero would always be the lean and daring outlaw, the fugitive who was never caught, the avenger of Southern rights, the fighter of the rich and their corporations, the Robin Hood. The hero would forever be Jesse James.

8

THE LEGEND THAT NEVER DIES

Much of the history of the West is wrapped in myth and tall stories. Jesse James was a towering figure. Writers and reporters took rumors and bits of truth about James and turned them into wild and fanciful tales.

There is a story about James when he was in western Missouri shortly after the Civil War. It seems the boys had just made a hit on a local bank. They were tired and hungry and stopped at a farmhouse for some food. A young widow answered James's knock on the door and invited the gang in for dinner. It turned out that her husband had been a Confederate soldier. The widow shared what food she had, and Jesse James handed her some money in return. But he noticed tears in her eyes. It seems that a banker was coming that very afternoon to foreclose on her farm. She had no money, and James was touched. He gave her several thousand dollars to pay off the entire mortgage. The woman was overcome with joy. After a couple of hours, the banker showed up ready to take over the property. The widow handed him the money and sent him on his way. As he headed down the road toward town, an armed man jumped in front of his horse and stole the money.[1] Yes, it was Jesse James!

The history of the West is also about the creation of heroes. In a period before sports figures, action heroes, and astronauts, certain individuals such as Jesse James satisfied the public's appetite for excitement and color, for violence and daring. At the hands of reporters, novelists, and advertisers, James became the image and symbol of masculinity, courage, defiance of authority, and ingenuity. He represented to many Americans the triumph of the common man over the establishment.

The Dime Novels

In the 1880s, one of the favorite forms of entertainment for the public was the dime novel. The books were short, inexpensive, and filled with wild tales of adventure. The dime novels, published in various sizes and formats, with print runs sometimes reaching over one hundred thousand, were popular for several decades.

The New York Detective Library published *The James Boys in a Fix*; Wide Awake Library presented *The James Boys' Bridges*; Log Cabin Library published *Jesse, the Outlaw: A Narrative of the James Boys by Capt. Jake Shackleford, the Western Detective*. For kids and their parents in New York or Indianapolis or Columbus, the West was only a dime novel away. In the West the mysterious forces of civilization and lawlessness were locked in a precarious battle. For a dime, you could get Jesse James. It was there that fact and fiction melted into one great glob of pulp fiction. It was there that the western outlaw hero was first mass-produced.

In 1915, when officers asked train robber Frank Ryan why he had turned from a life of respectability to that of a thief, he answered, "Bad companions and dime novels. Jesse James was my favorite hero. I used to read about him at school when us kids swapped dime novels." To make a name like James's, to leave behind the life of anonymity, to grab some quick bucks—the recipe was there in the little dog-eared dime novels, in their stories, songs, and poems.[2]

In the early 1880s, publishers featured the James gang in several dime novel series. The gang members were glorified as clever and courageous rebels fighting against the forces of power. The boys outwitted the big railroad tycoons, they defeated the thugs sent to destroy them, and they upheld the values of their own community.[3]

By the turn of the century, over two hundred seventy stories about Jesse James had made the pages of the pulp industry. Some were loosely based on fact, while others were totally imaginative. All were exaggerated. Jesse James became a symbol of manliness. He was tough, courageous, a fighter, able to get revenge against his enemies.

In the dime novels James became a national hero. Americans got to know him as a misunderstood trailblazer who was done in by treachery. He was portrayed as an heroic bad man of the plains, who stole horses, robbed stages, trains, and banks, mostly for honor and pride, not for money.

For Americans of all ages in the late nineteenth century, views of the West were largely shaped by the dime novels. They were also shaped by newspapers and magazines. Many Americans had never been in the West. They had never seen the prairies, deserts, or the giant Rocky Mountains. They had never seen badland towns, stagecoaches, American Indians, or bandits. For Americans who read the dime novels, Jesse James was mostly a dashing figure.

The Movies

Americans would soon begin to see Jesse James the outlaw from a wholly new perspective. They would not only learn about the daring outlaw in dime novels, but also see him in motion pictures.

In the movies, the entertainment invention for the twentieth century, Jesse James appeared as if in full life. All the excitement of the West—the danger of robberies, gunfights, and chases on horseback— was now on the screen. Moviegoers began to experience things about which they had only read. With the creation of the motion picture industry, the leap from crook to legend became far easier.

Hollywood has told and retold the story of Jesse James since the early days of the movie industry. The first film about Jesse James was made in 1920, a silent film called *Jesse James Under the Black Flag*. Somewhat uninspiring and dull, the movie flopped. But playing the lead was the famous outlaw's son, Jesse James, Jr.[4] Since then, at least twenty-five films have featured the adventures of Jesse James.

In 1927, Paramount Pictures released *Jesse James*, a silent film starring Fred Thompson and his famous horse, Silver King. The film, not surprisingly, presented Jesse James as a modern Robin Hood, a characterization in which Thompson himself thoroughly believed. He told a reporter from a Kansas City newspaper that James "was a strong, fearless man, without the trace of a mean trait." According to Thompson, James never robbed "the poor and needy."[5]

In 1939, Hollywood released *Jesse James*, a film directed by Henry King and starring two leading actors, Tyrone Power as Jesse and Henry Fonda as Frank James. The film portrayed Jesse James and his men as peaceful farmers thrust into outlawry by evil, grasping railroad owners who were taking over their lands. In order to sustain the heroic image of Jesse James, the film ignored James's murderous career as a Civil War guerrilla and as a bank robber. To evoke greater sympathy for the James character, the film depicted a gruesome murder of James's mother by hired railroad thugs. In real life, James's mother actually outlived her son by many years. But despite the inventions, the well-attended movie made the Jesse James myth come alive for many Americans.[6]

In 1980, United Artists released *The Long Riders*, yet another film on the James gang. Directed by Walter Hill, the film had a gimmick— the outlaw brothers were played by movie-actor brothers. The James brothers were played by Stacy and James Keach, the Younger brothers were played by Keith and Robert Carradine, and the Miller brothers were played by Randy and Dennis Quaid. Even the assassin brothers were played by brothers:

Christopher and Nicholas Guest played Charlie and Bob Ford.[7] Through the years, the Jesse James legend has consistently provided a popular storyline for the entertainment industry.

Jesse James as Inspiration

If the dime novels and the movies excited Americans across the country, they also gave a number of individuals a model on which to base their own lives. For some, Jesse James's life was inspiring. They wanted to be like James.

For this new generation of outlaws, the targets were still mostly banks, the teams were still small gangs, and the tactics were still the hit-and-run guerrilla methods employed half a century earlier. But the new generation had new tools. The horse had given way to the automobile.

To Charles "Pretty Boy" Floyd of Oklahoma, for example, Jesse James was an obsession. Floyd listened to aging farmers share insights about James's robberies and pestered his parents to buy books about the exploits of the famed Missouri outlaw. Floyd never tired of hearing the old stories. As he grew up, those stories became more than sources of amusement; they became blueprints for his own life.

Floyd publicly claimed to have robbed only wealthy men. Suddenly, this statement was in

A Nonviolent Outlaw

He was called Black Bart, but his real name was Charles E. Boles. A schoolteacher from California, Boles became one of the country's most celebrated stagecoach robbers. Between 1875 and 1883, Boles held up dozens of stages without firing a shot. Wearing a long coat and a flour sack over his head, he carried a shotgun but did not use it. He left short poems such as this one at the scene of the crimes:

Blame me not for what I've done
I don't deserve your curses,
And if for some cause I must be hung,
Let it be for my verses.

He was not hanged. When the Wells Fargo freight company finally captured him, they struck a deal. If he gave up the robbery business, Wells Fargo would give him a monthly pension. He accepted.[8]

articles across the country with apt comparisons—naturally—with Robin Hood and Jesse James.

Another notorious outlaw, Alvin Karpis, also wanted to be like Jesse James. As he fled from federal and state authorities in 1935, Karpis planned to rob a train, just like the great days on the frontier. Old Ben Grayson, a veteran bank robber who had been recently released from prison, was one of the first to hear of Karpis's plan. He was doubtful.

"Who . . . robs a train in this day and age?" Grayson asked quizzically. Later Karpis wrote, "I thought of the great bandits of the old West, the James brothers . . . and all the rest of them. They knocked over trains and I was going to pull the same stunt."[9]

He did. On the afternoon of November 7, 1935, five well-dressed men carrying machine guns robbed an Erie Railroad train at a station in Garrettsville, Ohio, east of Cleveland. Then they made off in a Plymouth sedan with nearly $45,000.[10] They left the state by plane. The afternoon newspaper called the caper "the daring Jesse James mail train robbery." Other newspapers also obligingly compared Karpis to Jesse James. He was pleased. He said, "I'd

The Dalton gang tried to do something the James boys had never done—rob two banks at the same time. Four of the gang died in Coffeyville, Kansas.

held up a train in fine style just like the famous old Western bandits."[11]

Keeping the Legend Alive

Through the years, Jesse James has continued to be in the news. In October 1927, in Kearney, Missouri, local townspeople debated whether to erect a monument to Jesse James. The idea ignited a national debate over the issue of this outlaw's special place in history. Why should the townspeople of his hometown glorify a crook? In *The New York Times*, a writer joked that the monument would rob the country of its favorite bandit. He would become respectable.[12]

On July 2, 1931, in the mountains near Wetmore, Colorado, a man named James Sears, who had lived as a hermit for many years, died. Shortly thereafter, William White, a friend of Sears's, revealed that the old loner had admitted to him that he was actually Jesse James and that the supposed killing of James a half century before had been a hoax perpetrated by the outlaw to escape punishment. The dead man in the ground in St. Joseph, Missouri, so the story went, was more than likely a member of the James gang who had died of typhoid fever.[13]

On April 21, 1932, in Excelsior Springs, Missouri, local citizens and Jesse James experts investigated the claims of another man who insisted he was James. Mrs. Jesse James, wife of the outlaw's son, who was in Missouri as an expert witness, produced one of Jesse James's boots for the test. When the man tried the shoe on, it did not fit.[14]

Through the years the stories continued. In 1940, a man named Lester B. Dill discovered some rusty guns and an old chest in one of the caves located on his property near Stanton, Missouri. Because of old stories about Jesse James using the cave as a hideout, Dill decided that the guns and chest had belonged to the famous outlaw. Dill soon put up a sign advertising the site and began to charge admission.[15]

In 1948, in Lawton, Oklahoma, two reporters for a local paper wrote a story claiming that James had not yet died. A man named J. Frank Dalton, about one hundred years old, they said, was actually the famous outlaw. The story claimed that this man had pulled off a great hoax. Supposedly, he had sung in the choir at his own funeral and had later graduated with honors under another alias at the University of Michigan. Soon, national moviegoers were in for a special historical treat.[16] In a Paramount Newsreel, the aged man was introduced.

The name of Jesse James was used commercially in almost any way imaginable. In 1966 Hollywood released *Jesse James Meets Frankenstein's Daughter*.[17]

At least in this case, no one appeared to believe that this particular story was based on fact.

On April 4, 1972, back in Kearney, Missouri, Fannie Shanks, a restaurant owner and promoter of the Jesse James Festival, explained to a reporter why she and other residents of the town were preparing to honor a criminal. "The James episode is part of history now," Fannie said. "Why not celebrate it with some square dances and shooting contests and the like?"[18] For Mina Spicer, longtime owner of the Kearney Variety Store, the whole James business was a bit weird: "Back in my day he was an outlaw. It was never talked about. For your kids growing up today it's history. They don't think of him as a bad guy. We did." Good or bad, Jesse James was honored by that day's festivities and the county restored his home.[19]

On May 24, 1981, in Liberty, Missouri, another monument to the life and deeds of Jesse James was erected. Town officials placed an inscribed bronze plaque on a two-story brick building. The inscription said that the building was the site of the first daylight bank holdup in United States history and that the 1866 robbery was pulled off by the James gang. It made little difference to townspeople in Liberty that historians had almost unanimously agreed that the robbery was certainly not perpetrated by Jesse James. Liberty's citizens

In the late twentieth century, many people, especially the descendants of the members of the James gang, wanted to remember the history and the legends surrounding the famous outlaws. This photo shows Bob, Jim, and Cole Younger with their sister, Henrietta, in 1889, a decade after their bank-robbing careers had ended.

wanted to be part of the legend. "Here is where America's greatest folklore history began and ended," said Milton Perry, Clay County superintendent of historical sites. "He's to this county what Robin Hood is to England."[20]

In September 1983, in Kearney, descendants of Frank and Jesse James and of Cole Younger and his brothers gathered for a weekend reunion. The relatives swapped stories and agreed on one thing—that history is flooded with misinformation about their famous kin.

Ninety years after his death, Jesse James still made a name for himself in Clay County and still brought out the crowds. Most of the people who had any dealings with the James family were long gone. But Grover Albright, a former postman and nearly ninety, remembered Jesse's brother, Frank James, in his last days. "Frank was one heck of a guy whenever I had any dealings with him," said Albright.[21]

9

THE JAMES LEGEND TODAY

When we think of bandits today, we think of the Old West, of train robberies, six-shooters, horses, and gunfights in dusty streets of frontier towns. We remember the legends—the heroes of dime novels and the romantic, misunderstood loners of the silver screen. We see Jesse James riding into Northfield. From novelists, journalists, historians, moviemakers, and singers, we have been showered with these images of Jesse James.

But if we stand back and get a fresh look, if we examine many of the old stories, and if we look at how the legends were formed and how the stories took on lives of their own, we can begin to see new dimensions.

Most of the hype, songs, and stories are mainly nonsense. But sing them and tell them again and again, and each time the deeds seem to become even more astonishing, the people even more romantic. New movies and new songs appear. The nation never seems to tire of Jesse James.

Throughout the nation, there are places devoted to keeping the Jesse James legend alive. The James house northeast of Kearney is still open for tours. Inside is the bed on which the brothers were born and a picture of Jesse James taken shortly before his death. Under the direction of a University of Missouri archaeologist, the outlaw's casket was moved from its former gravesite closer to the house. Other renovations of the farm have made the place even more inviting to tourists. Richard Weber, a local real estate agent and president of the Kearney Chamber of Commerce, believes that Jesse James can make Clay County an even more popular tourist attraction. "You can go anywhere and people have heard of Jesse James," he says.[1] The Jesse James festivals held in Kearney have included carnivals, parades, and the ever-popular mock bank robberies. Tourists substitute for the James gang, with guns (loaded with blanks) and money bags filled with

Another Bandit Hero

Another great bandit hero of the nineteenth century was Billy the Kid, whose real name was William Antrim. Billy was born shortly before the Civil War. His birthplace is still unknown. In his early teenage years, he worked on ranches and as a sheepherder. He took part in the Lincoln County, New Mexico, cattle war, and by 1880 he was one of the most wanted outlaws in the West. Like Jesse James, Billy's life story has been written and rewritten so many times that fact and fiction have become blurred. Also like James, he was a favorite figure of the dime novelists and moviemakers. He was also killed suddenly and without warning.

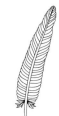

bubble gum, just trying to get a little closer to the legend.[2]

Many people over the years have refused to believe that Jesse James had actually been killed. James joined heroes from all ages and culture, from Russian czars to rock stars, who seem to escape death. For legends and folk heroes, this kind of survival in the face of all evidence is not unusual.

Shortly before he died in 1951, James's only known son, Jesse Edwards James, who had been in the house when his father was shot, said that twenty-six men had pretended to be his father. At least fifteen books had been written explaining how James had managed to escape his funeral. Aging hoaxers lugging old six-shooters gave lectures and personal appearances for money at tourist sites in the Midwest and West. There are people buried under headstones in Texas, Arkansas, and Missouri that bear the name of Jesse James.[3]

The closest known surviving blood relative of Jesse James is a man named James R. Ross, a retired judge in California. Jesse Edwards James was Ross's grandfather. Ross said, "My grandfather told me he ran into the house and saw his father lying on the floor with a bullet in his head and blood running out. All his life, my grandfather remembered that day."[4] Throughout his life, Ross has received letters from individuals who claim that Jesse James had not been killed. "I can't tell you how many people have sent me stupid letters. I have long wanted to have something that was really concrete that would shut these people up."[5]

In the summer of 1995, several hundred spectators gathered in a graveyard on a sweltering day in Kearney, Missouri. A few of the folks wore T-shirts bearing the words *We dig Jesse*. On that day, the body of the man in the grave of Jesse James was dug up by scientists to be tested to see if this was indeed the famous outlaw or someone else.

Jesse James lives on as one of the most memorable figures of the Old West.

The scientists, led by Professor James Starrs, exhumed the body in Missouri and subjected it to scientific tests. One hundred thirteen years after the original burial, samples from the body were compared with blood samples taken from James's descendants. They found out once and for all that the body was actually that of Jesse James.[6] The world was thus assured at last that James had, in fact, been killed. During James's reburial ceremonies on October 28, 1995, two men dressed in Confederate uniforms accompanied his casket.[7]

The heroic Jesse James still fills a public craving to see the triumph of man over his oppressors. He still fills a symbolic image of manliness and courage. Through the exploits of Jesse James, Americans experience the satisfaction of making a dramatic impact on society, if only in the pages of books or from a figure on the movie screen.

With each new treatment of his life on film, with each new song, with each new newspaper story, magazine article, and book, the dimensions of his character grow larger. To many Americans, the tales of Jesse James represent the highest standards of bravery and courage and honor. Over the years, Jesse James has remained an American hero, no matter what the truth.

CHRONOLOGY

1847—*September 5*: Jesse James is born in western Missouri.

1860—*December 20*: South Carolina leaves the Union.

1862—*January*: Frank James and Cole Younger join William Quantrill's raiders.

1863—*August 21*: Quantrill's guerrillas massacre citizens in Lawrence, Kansas.

1864—*May*: Jesse James joins guerrillas.

1864—*September 27*: Confederate guerrillas, led by Bloody Bill Anderson, loot and burn Centralia, Missouri; James brothers are part of raiding party.

1864—*October 27*: Bloody Bill Anderson killed; Jesse James swears revenge.

1865—*April 9*: Robert E. Lee surrenders to Ulysses S. Grant at Appomattox Court House; Civil War ends soon after.

1865—*May 10*: William Quantrill killed in Kentucky.

1866—*February 13*: Clay County Savings Bank in Liberty, Missouri, robbed.

1868—*March 20*: James gang robs Southern Deposit Bank in Russellville, Kentucky.

1869—*December 7*: James gang robs Daviess County Savings Bank in Gallatin, Missouri.

1871—*June 3*: James gang robs Ocobock Brothers' Bank in Corydon, Iowa.

1872—*September 26*: James gang robs Kansas City Fairgrounds.

1873—*July 21*: James gang commits its first train robbery near Adair, Iowa.

1874—*January 15*: James gang robs its first stagecoach.

1874—*January 31*: In Gads Hill, Missouri, James gang robs another train.

1874—*April 24*: Jesse James marries Zerelda (Zee) Mimms.

1875—*January 26*: Pinkertons raid James house and kill Jesse James's half brother.

1875—*December 31*: Zee James gives birth to Jesse Edwards James.

1876—*September 7*: James gang shot to pieces in Northfield, Minnesota.

1879—*July 17*: Zee James gives birth to Mary James.

1879—*October 8*: James gang holds up train in Glendale, Missouri.

1881—*July 15*: James gang robs train in Winston, Missouri.

1881—*September 7*: James gang robs train in Blue Cut, Missouri.

1882—*April 3*: Jesse James assassinated by Bob Ford.

CHAPTER NOTES

Chapter 1. "He Stopped the Glendale Train"
1. Richard Patterson, *Historical Atlas of the Outlaw West* (Boulder, Colo.: Johnson Books, 1985), p. 83.

Chapter 2. Growing Up in the Storm of War
1. Richard White, "Outlaw Gangs of the Middle Border: American Social Bandits," *The Western Historical Quarterly*, October 1981, p. 394.

2. William A. Settle, *Jesse James Was His Name* (Lincoln, Nebr.: University of Nebraska Press, 1966), p. 7.

3. Ibid.

4. Library of Congress, *American Memory Collections*, December 11, 1997, <http://www.loc.gov> (January 13, 1998).

5. Settle, p. 8.

6. Philip W. Steele, *The Many Faces of Jesse James* (Gretna, La.: Pelican Publishing Company, 1995), pp. 18–19.

7. "The James Gang Women," *Jesse James Home Page*, <http://www.m2computers.com/women2.html> (January 13, 1998).

8. Settle, p. 9.

9. Ibid., p. 10.

10. Thomas Goodrich, *Bloody Dawn: The Story of the Lawrence Massacre* (Kent, Ohio: The Kent State University Press, 1991), p. 7.

11. Peter Lyon, "The Wild, Wild West," *American Heritage*, August 1960, p. 39.

12. Settle, p. 14.

13. Ibid.

14. Ibid., pp. 18–19.

15. Leroy Fischer and Larry Rampp, "Quantrill's Civil War Operations in Indian Territory," *Chronicles of Oklahoma*, Summer 1968, p. 158.

16. Albert Castel, "William Clarke Quantrill: Terror of the Border," *Civil War*, January–February 1992, pp. 8–9.

17. Compiled Military Service Record, William Quantrill, Quantrill's Company Missouri (Confederate), National Archives, Washington, D.C.

18. Castel, p. 11.

19. Ibid., p. 22.

20. *The Gunfighters* (Alexandria, Va.: Time-Life Books, 1974), p. 56.

21. Marley Brant, *The Outlaw Youngers—A Confederate Brotherhood: A Biography* (Lanham, Md.: Madison Books, 1992), pp. 26–27.

22. White, p. 294.

23. Castel, p. 11.

24. Brant, pp. 30–31.

25. Goodrich, pp. 8–10.

26. Ibid., pp. 8–12.

27. Minnie B. Martin, Letter to her brother, December 25, 1863.

28. Goodrich, pp. 70–122.

29. Ibid., pp. 76–77.

30. Patricia Cassidy, "Bloody Kansas: Witnesses to Quantrill's Raid in Lawrence and Their Stories," *Civil War*, January–February 1922, p. 12; Goodrich, p. 107.

31. Goodrich, p. 124.

32. David Dary, *True Tales of the Old-Time Plains* (New York: Crown Publishers, 1979), p. 117.

33. Burton Williams, "Quantrill's Raid on Lawrence: A Question of Complicity," *Kansas Historical Quarterly*, 1968, p. 143.

34. Goodrich, p. 150.

35. E. B. Long, *The Civil War Day by Day: An Almanac* (Garden City: Doubleday & Company, 1971), p. 401.

36. Brant, p. 51.

37. Dary, p. 120.

38. Castel, p. 22.

39. Fischer and Rampp, pp. 160–165.

Chapter 3. The Boy Guerrilla Fighter

1. *The Gunfighters* (Alexandria, Va.: Time-Life Books, 1974), p. 56.

2. William A. Settle, *Jesse James Was His Name* (Lincoln, Nebr.: University of Nebraska Press, 1966), p. 27.

3. Marley Brant, *The Outlaw Youngers—A Confederate Brotherhood: A Biography* (Lanham, Md.: Madison Books, 1992), p. 57.

4. Albert Castel, "William Clarke Quantrill," *Civil War*, January–February 1992, p. 12.

5. Thomas Goodrich, *Bloody Dawn: The Story of the Lawrence Massacre* (Kent, Ohio: The Kent State University Press, 1991), p. 180.

6. Castel, p. 12.

7. Blaine Harden, "Wanted," *The Washington Post Magazine*, November 19, 1995, p. 25.

8. "Sketch of the Marauder Quantrill and His Operation," *The New York Times*, March 26, 1865, p. 3.

9. Brant, p. 59.

10. E. B. Long, *The Civil War Day by Day: An Almanac* (Garden City: Doubleday & Company, 1971), p. 687.

11. Castel, p. 12.

12. Ibid.; *The Gunfighters*, p. 56.

13. Burton Williams, "Quantrill's Raid on Lawrence: A Question of Complicity," *Kansas Historical Quarterly*, 1968, p. 143.

Chapter 4. The Rise of the Bandit King

1. Richard White, "Outlaw Gangs of the Middle Border: American Social Bandits," *The Western Historical Quarterly*, October 1981, p. 397.

2. *The Gunfighters* (Alexandria, Va.: Time-Life Books, 1974), p. 59.

3. William A. Settle, *Jesse James Was His Name* (Lincoln, Nebr.: University of Nebraska Press, 1969), p. 32.

4. "Clay County Savings Association Bank, Liberty, Missouri," *James–Younger Gang Home Page*, October 14, 1997, <http://www.islandnet.com/~the-gang/clay.htm> (January 14, 1998).

5. Ibid.

6. Marley Brant, *The Outlaw Youngers—A Confederate Brotherhood: A Biography* (Lanham, Md.: Madison Books, 1992), p. 71.

7. Richard Patterson, *Historical Atlas of the Outlaw West* (Boulder, Colo.: Johnson Books, 1985), p. 87; Castel, p. 12.

8. Settle, pp. 35–36.

9. "Clay County Savings Association Bank, Liberty, Missouri," *James–Younger Gang Home Page*.

10. Philip Steele, "Nimrod Long & Co., Bank, Russellville, Kentucky," *James–Younger Gang Home Page*, October 14, 1997, <http://www.islandnet.com/~the-gang/nimrod.htm> (January 14, 1998).

11. Ibid.

12. Albert Castel, "William Clarke Quantrill," *Civil War*, January–February 1992, p. 12.

13. Brant, pp. 73–75.

14. Settle, p. 36.

15. Ibid.

16. Brant, pp. 80–82.

17. Ibid., p. 88.

18. Patterson, p. 82; Castel, p. 15.

19. *The Gunfighters*, p. 62.

20. Brant, p. 22.

21. Patterson, p. 84.

22. Library of Congress, *American Memory Collections*, December 11, 1997, <http://www.loc.gov> (January 13, 1998).

23. Settle, p. 45.

24. Castel, p. 15.

25. Richard White, "Outlaw Gangs of the Middle Border: American Social Bandits," *The Western Historical Quarterly*, October 1981, p. 403.

26. *The Gunfighters*, pp. 62–63.

27. Blaine Harden, "Wanted," *The Washington Post Magazine*, November 19, 1995, p. 25.

28. Richard Slotkin, *Gunfighter Nation: The Myth of the Frontier in Twentieth-Century America* (New York: HarperPerennial, 1992), p. 135.

29. Library of Congress, *American Memory Collections*.

30. Harden, pp. 20–21; White, p. 390.

31. Library of Congress, *American Memory Collections*.

Chapter 5. Train Robbing

1. Richard Patterson, *Historical Atlas of the Outlaw West* (Boulder, Colo.: Johnson Books, 1985), p. 57; Marley Brant, *The Outlaw Youngers—A Confederate Brotherhood: A Biography* (Lanham, Md.: Madison Books, 1992), pp. 121–122.

2. "Chicago, Rock Island & Pacific Railroad Train Robbery, Adair, Iowa," *James–Younger Gang Home Page*, October 14, 1997, <http://www.islandnet.com/~the gang/chicago1.htm> (January 14, 1998).

3. "Hot Springs Stage Robbery," *James–Younger Gang Home Page*, October 14, 1997, <http://www.islandnet.com/~the-gang/stage1.htm> (January 14, 1998).

4. Patterson, p. 82.

5. *The Gunfighters* (Alexandria, Va.: Time-Life Books, 1974), p. 67.

6. Brant, pp. 128–129.

7. Richard Slotkin, *Gunfighter Nation: The Myth of the Frontier in Twentieth-Century America* (New York: HarperPerennial, 1992), pp. 136–137.

8. William A. Settle, *Jesse James Was His Name* (Lincoln, Nebr.: University of Nebraska Press, 1966), p. 49.

9. Peter Lyon, "The Wild, Wild West," *American Heritage*, August 1960, p. 33.

10. Albert Castel, "William Clarke Quantrill," *Civil War*, January–February 1992, p. 15.

11. Frederick Voss and James Barber, *We Never Sleep: The First Fifty Years of the Pinkertons* (Washington, D.C.: Smithsonian Institution Press, 1981), pp. 6–7.

12. Ibid., pp. 12–13.

13. *The Gunfighters*, p. 67.

14. Brant, pp. 130–131.

15. Ibid., pp. 137–138.

16. Settle, pp. 69–70.

17. Ibid.

18. Ibid., pp. 76–77.

19. "The James Boys: The Attempt to Capture Them at Kearny," *The New York Times*, February 1, 1875, p. 2.

20. Settle, pp. 77–78.

21. Ibid., p. 78.
22. "The Capture of the James Boys," *The New York Times,* January 29, 1875, p. 1.
23. Settle, pp. 80–81.
24. Brant, pp. 154–157.
25. James D. Horan, *The Pinkertons: The Detective Dynasty That Made History* (New York: Bonanza Books, 1967), p. 201.
26. Settle, p. 105.

Chapter 6. The Northfield Disaster

1. Northfield News Publishing, Inc., "The Northfield Bank Raid," *Northfield Home Page,* n.d., <http://www.northfield.org/jj/raid book.htm> (January 14, 1998).
2. Ibid.
3. Marley Brant, *The Outlaw Youngers—A Confederate Brotherhood: A Biography* (Lanham, Md.: Madison Books, 1992), pp. 176–179.
4. Northfield News Publishing, Inc., *Northfield Home Page.*
5. Ibid.
6. Ibid.
7. Albert Castel, "William Clarke Quantrill," *Civil War,* January–February 1992, p. 16; Brant, p. 183.
8. James D. Horan, *The Pinkertons: The Detective Dynasty That Made History* (New York: Bonanza Books, 1967), p. 191.
9. Northfield News Publishing, Inc., *Northfield Home Page.*
10. Brant, pp. 194–197.
11. William A. Settle, *Jesse James Was His Name* (Lincoln, Nebr.: University of Nebraska Press, 1966), p. 93.
12. Brant, p. 203.
13. *The Gunfighters* (Alexandria, Va.: Time-Life Books, 1974), p. 80.

Chapter 7. Taking Jesse James Down

1. Philip W. Steele, *The Many Faces of Jesse James* (Gretna, La.: Pelican Publishing Company, 1995), pp. 33–45.
2. Marley Brant, *The Outlaw Youngers—A Confederate Brotherhood: A Biography* (Lanham, Md.: Madison Books, 1992), pp. 312–313.
3. "Daughter of Jesse James Returns to Pay a Visit to Place of Her Birth," *Nashville Banner,* April 3, 1933; Brant, p. 219.
4. Brant, p. 219.
5. William A. Settle, *Jesse James Was His Name* (Lincoln, Nebr.: University of Nebraska Press, 1966), p. 108.
6. *The Gunfighters* (Alexandria, Va.: Time-Life Books, 1974), p. 82.
7. Settle, p. 107.
8. Ibid., pp. 110–111.

9. Ibid., p. 112.

10. Ibid.

11. Blaine Harden, "Wanted," *The Washington Post Magazine*, November 19, 1995, p. 24; Richard Patterson, *Historical Atlas of the Outlaw West* (Boulder, Colo.: Johnson Books, 1985), p. 90; Brant, pp. 223–224.

12. Alan Lomax, *The Folk Songs of North America* (New York: Doubleday and Company, 1960), pp. 351–352.

13. Harden, p. 24.

14. Settle, p. 119.

15. "Justice for Jesse?" n.d., <http://www.cam.org/~charlie/jesse> (February 10, 1998).

16. Settle, p. 120.

17. Ibid., p. 126.

18. Lomax, p. 346.

19. Settle, p. 175.

20. Brant, pp. 224–225.

21. Patterson, p. 36.

22. James D. Horan, *The Pinkertons: The Detective Dynasty That Made History* (New York: Bonanza Books, 1967), p. 325.

23. Castel, p. 17.

24. "To Surpass Jesse James: Why the Dalton Gang Made the Coffeyville Raid," *The New York Times*, October 7, 1892, p. 5.

25. Patterson, p. 85.

26. Castel, p. 18.

27. Brant, p. 297.

28. Ibid., p. 299.

Chapter 8. The Legend That Never Dies

1. "Daughter of Jesse James Returns to Pay a Visit to Place of Her Birth," *Nashville Banner*, April 3, 1933; William A. Settle, *Jesse James Was His Name* (Lincoln, Nebr.: University of Nebraska Press, 1966), pp. 171–172.

2. Christine Bold, *Selling the West: Popular Western Fiction, 1860–1960* (Bloomington, Ind.: Indiana University Press, 1987), pp. 2–6; Roger Bruns, *The Bandit Kings: From Jesse James to Pretty Boy Floyd* (New York: Crown Publishers, 1995), p. 146.

3. Richard Slotkin, *Gunfighter Nation: The Myth of the Frontier in Twentieth-Century America* (New York: HarperPerennial, 1992), p. 138.

4. Northfield News Publishing, Inc., *Northfield Home Page*, "Celluloid Slant: Hollywood Has Wide Variety of Films About Jesse James," n.d., <http:// www.northfield.org/jj/jjfilm.htm> (January 14, 1998).

5. Settle, pp. 177–178.

6. Slotkin, p. 295–301.

7. Northfield News Publishing, Inc., *Northfield Home Page*.

8. Leonard Weisenberg, "They Also Rode," *Cobblestone*, May 1996, pp. 31–32.

9. Alvin Karpis, *The Alvin Karpis Story* (New York: Coward, McCann and Geoghegan, Inc., 1971), pp. 209–210.

10. Ibid.

11. Ibid., p. 218.

12. *The New York Times*, September 18, 1927.

13. Settle, pp. 169–170.

14. Ibid.

15. Michael Wallis, *Route 66: The Mother Road* (New York: St. Martin's Press, 1990), p. 63.

16. Ibid., p. 67.

17. Northfield News Publishing, Inc., *Northfield Home Page*.

18. B. Drummond Ayres, Jr., "In Frank and Jesse James Country, the Passage of Time Finds a Town Ready to Forgive—And Cash In," *The New York Times*, April 5, 1972, p. 31.

19. Ibid.

20. *The New York Times*, May 24, 1981.

21. *Arizona Daily Star*, September 18, 1983.

Chapter 9. The James Legend Today

1. *The New York Times*, May 24, 1981.

2. Ibid.

3. Blaine Harden, "Wanted," *The Washington Post Magazine*, November 19, 1995, p. 26.

4. Ibid.

5. Ibid.

6. Ibid., pp. 19–26.

7. "The Ballad of Jesse and John," *The Economist*, December 2, 1995, p. 25.

GLOSSARY

badman—A tough guy; a ruffian; a gunman; a killer.

Colt—Six-shooter revolving pistol made by Samuel Colt; the West's most popular pistol in the nineteenth century.

deputy—A sheriff's assistant or second in command who can act in place of the sheriff.

dime novel—One of the short pieces of adventure fiction published in the latter half of the nineteenth century.

guerrilla—A member of a small force of soldiers, usually volunteers, making surprise, quick-strike raids.

jayhawker—A member of a band of antislavery guerrillas in Kansas and Missouri before and during the Civil War.

lynch—To kill, usually by hanging, someone suspected of a crime.

outlaw—A criminal.

Pinkerton—A detective of the Pinkerton agency, organized in Chicago in 1850 by Allan Pinkerton.

posse—A group of riders brought together by a law officer to track down an outlaw.

sheriff—Elected law enforcement officer of a county.

Smith & Wesson—A pistol invented by gunsmiths Horace Smith and Daniel Wesson and made in Springfield, Massachusetts.

stagecoach—An enclosed, horse-drawn vehicle of public transportation. Stagecoaches were favorite targets of outlaws.

vigilante—A citizen who takes the law into his or her own hands to punish a criminal.

Wild West show—An outdoor entertainment with such exhibitions as shooting, riding, roping, and fake robberies.

FURTHER READING

Adams, Ramon. *Burrs Under the Saddle: A Second Look at Books and Histories of West*. Norman: University of Oklahoma Press, 1964.

Bold, Christine. *Selling the Wild West: Popular Western Fiction, 1860–1960*. Bloomington: Indiana University Press, 1987.

Brant, Marley. *The Outlaw Youngers—A Confederate Brotherhood: A Biography*. Lanham, Md.: Madison Books, 1992.

Breihan, Carl W. *Lawmen and Robbers*. Caldwell, Ida.: The Caxton Printers, Ltd., 1986.

Bruns, Roger. *The Bandit Kings: From Jesse James to Pretty Boy Floyd*. New York: Crown Publishers, 1995.

Dary, David. *True Tales of the Old-Time Plains*. New York: Crown Publishers, 1979.

Goodrich, Thomas. *Bloody Dawn: The Story of the Lawrence Massacre*. Kent, Ohio: Kent State University Press, 1991.

Green, Carl R., and William R. Sanford. *Jesse James*. Springfield, N.J.: Enslow Publishers, Inc., 1992.

The Gunfighters. Alexandria, Va.: Time-Life Books, 1974.

Horan, James D. *The Pinkertons: The Detective Dynasty That Made History*. New York: Bonanza Books, 1967.

Patterson, Richard. *Historical Atlas of the Outlaw West*. Boulder, Colo.: Johnson Books, 1985.

Pinkerton, William. *Train Robberies and Train Robbers*. Fort Davis, Tex.: Frontier Book Co., 1968.

Rosa, Joseph G. *The Gunfighter: Man or Myth?* Norman: University of Oklahoma Press, 1969.

Settle, William A. *Jesse James Was His Name*. Lincoln: University of Nebraska Press, 1966.

Slotkin, Richard. *Gunfighter Nation: The Myth of the Frontier in Twentieth-Century America*. New York: HarperPerennial, 1992.

Steckmesser, Kent L. *The Western Hero in History and Legend*. Norman: University of Oklahoma Press, 1965.

Steele, Philip W. *The Many Faces of Jesse James*. Gretna, La.: Pelican Publishing Company, 1995.

Tatum, Stephen. *Inventing Billy the Kid: Visions of the Outlaw in America, 1881–1981*. Albuquerque: University of New Mexico Press, 1982.

INDEX